Arcadia Updated

Arcadia Updated delves into the concept of landscape as it is shaped by the literary tradition and material works known as pastoral. Referring to several of the tradition's works as well as scholarly critiques, Fiskevold and Geelmuyden highlight how individual landscape perception is primarily a cultural construct: each individual may see a unique landscape based on personal experiences, but simultaneously, *landscape* represents a tradition of engaging with nature and land, which has been largely forgotten. In re-engaging and connecting the practice of understanding landscapes with the pastoral tradition, the authors establish a common ground for treating landscape as an object of analysis in landscape planning. *Arcadia Updated* contributes to the methodological debate concerning landscape character assessment.

Including 30 black-and-white images, this book analyses how humans engage with land organically, materially and communicatively. It seeks to raise landscape awareness as both an individual and a collective act of imagination. The practice of analysing landscapes is an ongoing culture of reinterpreting the land as landscape in response to society's development and technical progress. The role of the landscape analyst is to interpret the contemporary world and offer visual explanations of it.

This book will be beneficial to professional landscape planners as well as to academics and students of landscape, literature and cultural studies. It provides an essential contribution to the cross-disciplinarity of the landscape discourse.

Marius Fiskevold received a Cand. Agric. in landscape architecture from the Agricultural University of Norway in 1998. He worked as a landscape designer and planner for a number of consulting companies for 10 years before starting a PhD study, which he finished in 2012 with a thesis entitled "The road as will and representation: landscape analysis and aesthetic experience". In addition to his work as a landscape architect and planner, he draws heavily on his long experience with and passion for landscape photography. All the original photographs in this book are his. He now works as a landscape architect at Sweco Norge AS and as an assistant professor at the School of Landscape Architecture at the Norwegian University of Life Sciences (NMBU).

Anne Katrine Geelmuyden received a Cand. Agric. in landscape architecture from the Agricultural University of Norway in 1982. She gained a PhD from the same university in 1989 with a thesis entitled "Landscape experience and landscape: ideology or critique of ideology?", an early example of the social constructivist approach in landscape studies, at least within landscape architecture. She works as a professor at NMBU, where she heads the programme board at the School of Landscape Architecture. Her research focuses on the conceptualisation of landscape, landscape aesthetics and landscape criticism.

Arcadia Updated

Raising landscape awareness through analytical narratives

Marius Fiskevold and Anne Katrine Geelmuyden

Routledge
Taylor & Francis Group

LONDON AND NEW YORK

First published 2019
by Routledge
2 Park Square, Milton Park, Abingdon, Oxon OX14 4RN

and by Routledge
605 Third Avenue, New York, NY 10017

First issued in paperback 2022

Routledge is an imprint of the Taylor & Francis Group, an Informa business

British Library Cataloguing-in-Publication Data
A catalogue record for this book is available from the British Library

Library of Congress Cataloging-in-Publication Data
Names: Fiskevold, Marius, 1973– author. | Geelmuyden, Anne Katrine, author.
Title: Arcadia updated : raising landscape awareness through analytical narratives / Marius Fiskevold and Anne Katrine Geelmuyden.
Description: New York : Routledge, 2019. |
Includes bibliographical references and index.
Identifiers: LCCN 2018023959 | ISBN 9781138496941 (hardback) |
ISBN 9780429466441 (ebook)
Subjects: LCSH: Landscapes. | Landscapes in art. | Landscapes in literature.
Classification: LCC BH301.L3 F57 2019 | DDC 712–dc23
LC record available at https://lccn.loc.gov/2018023959

ISBN: 978-1-03-240177-5 (pbk)
ISBN: 978-1-138-49694-1 (hbk)
ISBN: 978-0-429-46644-1 (ebk)

DOI: 10.4324/9780429466441

Typeset in Sabon
by Out of House Publishing

Contents

List of figures   vii
Preface   ix

1   Introduction: reinterpreting landscapes in an evolving world   1
    Raising landscape awareness through analytical landscape
        narratives 2
    Sustaining the poetic potential of landscapes through action 3
    Activating and actualising the landscape ideal of the insider 9

2   The pastoral tradition as inherited motives   15
    Pastoral attitude and visual rationality 15
    Shared appearances: the constructive act of seeing 16
    Enlightening discrepancy: the dialectic act of seeing 21
    Subjective emancipation: the revelatory act of seeing 26

3   From classical pastorals to pastoral landscapes:
    rebirth of the landscape as fragile nature   33
    Et in Arcadia ego 1999 33
    Landscape as cultural idea: image of unity between humanity
        and nature 36
    Pastoral motives invested in modern pastoral landscapes 39
    From sight to insight: methodological liminality 45
    Contemporary pastoral analytical narration 50

4   Instances of pastoral motivation in contemporary
    landscape analytical practice   61
    Creating landscapes within the analytical narrative's horizon of
        comprehension 61

*Vegaøyan: exposing a World Heritage landscape through the
  lens of an analytical narrative* 63
Sarpefossen: extracting a poetic landscape from an ordinary area 68
Subjective emancipation: translating awareness into identity 75
The action *of the landscape analyst offers an invitation to
  inhabit an image* 81

5   Articulating analytical narratives of contemporary
    pastoral landscapes   85
    From human activity to landscapes of reflection 85
    Edelgranveien as articulated landscape 89
    The material landscape of Vækerø 98
    The organic landscape of Kustein 110
    Land reflected as landscapes 120

6   The landscape analyst's pastoral *action*   125
    Computed landscapes 125
    The visual rationality of analytical narratives 129

    Glossary   139
    Index   141

Figures

1.1 Christian Skredsvig's painting "The Boy with the Willow Flute", signposted at the picnic site by Dælivannet in Bærum municipality as visual reference   7

2.1 The symbolic event of seeing traced from the moment of attention to the area down to a gesturing landscape utterance   17

2.2 Poussin, *Et in Arcadia ego*, first (Chatsworth) version   22

2.3 Poussin, *Et in Arcadia ego*, second (Louvre) version   23

4.1 Vega   63

4.2 Sarpefossen   70

4.3 Map of Sarpefossen   71

4.4 Landscape formation extended with analytical terminology. The "input" is features of the land perceived as indicators of a concept. The product is a motif. The "output" is the significance and location of the motif   72

4.5 Walking on thin ice in the landscape of Storhei   80

5.1 Wet snowfall on Edelgranveien   90

5.2 Roadside weeds   91

5.3 Slush at a road crossing   92

5.4 Melting snow   93

5.5 Black tarmac   94

5.6 Ski tracks on the roadside   96

5.7 Crossing the snowbank   97

5.8 Steps down to the shore at Vækerø   100

5.9 Entrance plaza at Vækerø   101

5.10 Promenade along the shore at Vækerø   102

5.11 Boardwalk passing a steep cliff   103

5.12 Pedestrian tunnel   104

5.13 Motorway corridor   106

5.14 Reefs   107

5.15 Terrace between Vækerø manor house and the seashore   108

5.16 Sculpted water channel   110

5.17   Rambler's view of the trunks and foliage   112
5.18   Melting tarn   113
5.19   Snowstorm gradually effacing ski tracks   114
5.20   Huge masses of snow   115
5.21   Ski track in sunny weather   116
5.22   Snow transforms the forest ground into a floor   118
5.23   Logging machine   119
5.24   Pastoral motives and landscapes of reflection condense and
       separate in the motifs of a narrative   122

Preface

Landscapes can never be seen; they are always products of our imagination. When we speak with each other about a landscape, or even when we just observe a piece of land, our individual seeing is guided by cognition and memory. They equip us with a culturally inherited idea that we know as *landscape,* and which helps us to imaginatively recognise and assemble a unique visual entity from the chaos of an area's features. Leaving out some and highlighting others, we endow our vision with meaning in accordance with a current engagement with the land. One fundamental source of landscape meaning is the tradition of cultural pastorals in Western art. As pastoral heritage, any landscape is imbued with humans' dreams and aspirations concerning the relationship between humanity and nature. The literary scholar Jonathan Bate (Bate, 2000:ix) has characterised writing in the pastoral tradition poetically as "the capacity of the writer to restore us to the earth which is our home". In these chapters, *pastoral* implies a relationship that is both light and dark at the same time. Imaging a landscape is a way of seeing the land, which creatively plays out humanity's existential liminality in relation to nature as the distinctly Other. It is a world where humans can develop their passion for belonging.

In this book we follow up and develop thoughts that we presented in our doctoral theses in landscape architecture, published 22 years apart in Norwegian, at the Norwegian University of Life Sciences. Both theses dealt theoretically with the problems of analysing landscapes. Geelmuyden's thesis (Geelmuyden, 1989) was an early attempt to incorporate into landscape analysis practice the cultural constructivist approach to landscape that was being developed mostly in cultural geography. Combining that approach with critical hermeneutics, especially *The theory of communicative action* by Jürgen Habermas (Habermas, 1984), she posited landscape planning as an exercise of *communicative rationality*. This meant a critical attitude towards the lack of theoretical underpinnings for evaluation criteria within landscape architecture, but it did not arrive at any foundation for the intersubjective "everyday sense of truth, justice and sincerity"

(Geelmuyden, 1989:112) other than dialogue. Two decades later, within a different political, philosophical, and landscape theory and practice context, Fiskevold's thesis (Fiskevold, 2011) examined how the European Landscape Convention's relativistic definition of landscape as "an area as perceived by people" and its declaration of landscape as a "common good" could be combined in a method for landscape characterisation. He established a basic terminology for analysing landscapes. A landscape is an individual's *image* of the land; this image can be characterised by its *horizons* of motion and comprehension it is *motivated* in an actual human practice, where it becomes manifest as *motifs* in *utterances*, such as for instance landscape analyses.

Both theses were united in placing landscape architecture within the humanities. Landscape architecture's field of action aligns itself with humanities disciplines and critical practices that study humanity's relation to nature and create works that cultivate this relationship through artistic production, design and philosophical reflection. Its quintessential form of expression is the garden and garden theory. Today, the practice of cultivating the relationship between humanity and nature aesthetically also shows itself in the way landscape architects and planners display landscapes, for instance through landscape analyses.

This book provides a theory and value base for analytical practice in landscape planning. Methodologically, it presents an opposition to positivistic approaches to landscape research such as those in environmental psychology, health studies or landscape ecology.

We take further Fiskevold's terminology, combining it with recent scholarly interpretations of pastoral literature and painting, to develop a strategy and conceptual framework for landscape characterisation through *analytical narratives*. We emphasise two aspects of analytical landscape narration. First, we place the practice of analysing landscapes within the realm of societal discourse. This involves taking a position regarding the relationship between humans and their ever more digitally programmed environment. In planning, this means taking a public position about an area's *potential for appearing* as an aesthetically coherent, diverse and unique entity at any specific time and place. Thus, notions of power, truth and democratic exchange between multiple perceptions and voices are automatically implicated. Second, we therefore attach our reflections to the philosopher Hannah Arendt's idea of human *action* carried out in a *polis*, the ideal site of political interaction. Like Habermas, she conceives of power as the ability to agree upon a common course of action in unconstrained communication, but more than Habermas, she recognises that decision-making processes must sustain and encourage a plurality of voices in modern democracies, even at the cost of predictability and fixed and ideal rationality rationality (Plot, 2009). Accordingly, we embed landscape analyses within the *visual rationality* of what we have called a *polis of the eye*. By fusing contemporary practices with three essential motives in the pastoral tradition, our aim is to reinstate aesthetics as an essential and legitimising part of landscape planning.

In order to be shareable among a group of people as well as conceivable by each individual, a landscape image must be proposed by the landscape analyst through a publicly uttered analytical narrative. This act of "educated imagination", in literary scholar Northrop Frye's precise expression, is part and parcel of being able to *present* a visible and symbolic landscape to others (Frye, 1964). Most importantly, in this age of increasing computation and regulation of all realms of human life, we advocate analytical narratives as a poetic-rhetorical way of engaging people in imagining the land as landscapes, places where the individual can exercise the right to inhabit the world on his or her own unique terms.

References

Bate, J. 2000. *The song of the earth*, London, Picador.

Fiskevold, M. 2011. *Veien som vilje og forestilling: analysemetoder for landskap og estetisk erfaring*, Ås, Universitetet for miljø- og biovitenskap.

Frye, N. 1964. *The educated imagination*, Bloomington, Indiana University Press.

Geelmuyden, A. K. 1989. *Landskapsopplevelse og landskap: ideologi eller ideologikritikk? Et essay om de teoretiske vilkårene for vurdering av landskap i arealplanleggingen*, Ås, Institutt for landskapsarkitektur.

Habermas, J. 1984. *The theory of communicative action 1: reason and the rationalization of society*, London, Heinemann.

Plot, M. 2009. Communicative action's democratic deficit: a critique of Habermas's contribution to democratic theory. *International Journal of Communication*, 3, 825–852.

Chapter 1

Introduction

Reinterpreting landscapes in an evolving world

Box 1.1

Tonen

I skogen smågutten gik dagen lang,
gik dagen lang,
der havde han hørt slig en underlig sang,
underlig sang.

Gutten en fløjte af selje skar,
af selje skar, –
og prøvde, om tonen derinne var,
derinne var.

Tonen, den hvisked og nævnte sig,
og nævnte sig;
men bedst som han lydde, den løb sin vej,
den løb sin vej.

Tidt, når han sov, den til ham smøg,
den til ham smøg.
Og over hans pande med elskov strøg,
med elskov strøg.

Vilde den fange og vågned brat,
og vågned brat;
men tonen hang fast i den blege nat,
i den blege nat.

«Herre min Gud, tag mig derind,
tag mig derind;
ti tonen har fået mit hele sind,
mit hele sind.»

Herren, han svared: «den er din ven;
den er din ven;
skønt aldrig en time du ejer den,
du ejer den.»

The Melody

The youth in the woods spent the whole day long,
The whole day long;
For there he had heard such a wonderful song,
Wonderful song.

Willow-wood gave him a flute so fair,
A flute so fair,--
To try, if within were the melody rare,
Melody rare.

Melody whispered and said: "I am here!"
Said: "I am here!"
But while he was listening, it fled from his ear,
Fled from his ear.

Oft when he slept, it to him crept,
It to him crept;
And over his forehead in love it swept,
In love it swept.

When he would seize it, his sleep took flight,
His sleep took flight;
The melody hung in the pallid night,
In the pallid night.

"Lord, O my God, take me therein,
Take me therein!
The melody rare all my soul doth win,
My soul doth win."

Answered the Lord: "'T is your friend alone,
Your friend alone;
Though never an hour you it shall own,
You it shall own." _

TRANSLATED FROM THE NORWEGIAN IN THE ORIGINAL METERS
BY ARTHUR HUBBELL PALMER
Professor of the German Language and Literature In Yale
University

New York
The American-Scandinavian Foundation
London: Humphrey Milford
Oxford University Press
1915

Raising landscape awareness through analytical landscape narratives

The excerpt from the poem *Tonen* (*The Melody*) by the Norwegian poet Bjørnstjerne Bjørnson (Bjørnson, 1915) gives us a glimpse into humankind's poetic engagement with the environment. This instance of *pastoral art* in Western culture motivates the following chapters. The pastoral tradition dates as far back as to the *Idylls* of the Greek poet Theocritus (ca. 305–250 BCE) and plays a major role in the development of our contemporary Western concept of *landscape* (Hunt, 1992:50; Ruff, 2015). Hesiod's *Works and Days* (ca. 700 BCE) is said to have inspired Theocritus' *Idylls*, which in turn served as a model for Roman poets such as Vergil and Horace. These first codifications of the coexistence between humanity and nature were revived in the Italian Renaissance and subsequently carried over into the literature, visual arts and garden design of the 16th and 17th centuries. During this period, a vast number of pastoral works were able to continuously reinvest the myth of a distant Arcadia with contemporary significance. Through reflective narration and the imaginative reinterpretation of well-known motifs shared by different religions, nations and cultures, a great variety of landscapes were created.

Over the last centuries, however, all traces of the pastoral tradition appear to have been wiped out of the human approach to cultural landscapes in planning (Cosgrove, 1998; Andrews, 1999). The once widespread cultural convention of expressing emotional attachment to nature, as well as reflecting on one's own or one's fellow humans' struggles and successes, through communally understood pastoral narratives seems to have disappeared from the arena of public discourse. There may be two interrelated reasons for this. First, the reinterpretation of the myth of Arcadia has been reduced to the rendering of scenic clichés, uncritically reproduced as a sign of taste and class belonging. The reputation of the tradition itself is that it is a shallow and outdated genre (Williams, 1993; Olwig, 1996; Cosgrove, 1998). In landscape planning, the term "pastoral" has similarly been used derogatorily, denoting a superficially scenic, illusory or outdated ideal (Weller, 2006:73; Corner, 1999:156). Second, the continuation of cultural pastoralism has been disconnected from and denied its most powerful means of expression: humanity's innate *aesthetic* engagement with nature has been expelled from the public arena for a long time (Geelmuyden, 1993, 1989a, 1989b).

In this situation of apparent decline, we argue that the pastoral tradition still is one of what French philosopher Jean-François Lyotard (Lyotard, 1984) has termed our culture's "grand narratives". Disguised as "sustainability" or, as the European Landscape Convention puts it, "a key element of individual and social well-being" (Council of Europe, 2000:Preamble), it lives on in a contemporary version. These newer manifestations of the Arcadian myth, however, differ in a crucial way from the old ones in that they fail to address explicitly visual and emotional aspects of human engagement with land. Although inherited pastoral motifs can sometimes still be found serving as implicit references in landscape analyses and evaluations, the tradition's motivation has mostly been transformed to fit bureaucratic goals for efficient place production through a quasi-scientific methodology.

Arcadia Updated reaches back to the symbolic origins of the pastoral tradition and demonstrates how their underlying motivation can shape a critical language for analysing landscapes in a democratic planning discourse. Despite its references to land and land features, a landscape analysis moves entirely within the realm of language: in a mutual exchange and interplay between land, images and words, the entire process of landscape formation is tied to the constitutive conditions and character of its verbal utterance. In a reflective and narrative move analogous to the poem's above, the voice of the analyst must turn the sounds of the ever-evolving world into comprehensible melodies, contemporary landscape analytical narratives (Hunt, 2000).

We argue for a hermeneutic approach rather than a positivistic one as the most appropriate for meeting the European Landscape Convention's aim to raise landscape awareness. Every single individual sees its environment in a unique way. But instead of highlighting these differences as the problem in landscape planning (Jones, 2007; Jones et al., 2011), we have chosen to emphasise and explore the commonalities of landscape perception. This book shows that a shared landscape requires and implies a collective act of imagination. In planning, it is led by an expert and uttered through an analytical narrative. Raising landscape awareness means making visible a piece of land under a current circumstance, thus making it available for shared recognition and comprehension following the visual rationality of an analytical narrative. Through the voice of the analyst, contemporary human engagement with land can be translated into visible and potentially shared motifs that are perceivable by any attentive reader of the analytical narrative (Fiskevold, 2011).

Sustaining the poetic potential of landscapes through *action*

An interpretation of the poem *Tonen* reveals many of the complexities attached to the visual rationality of an analytical narrative. We interpret the poem as a form of analytical narrative, and we shall emphasise its calling for subjective *imagination*, traditional *pastoral motivation* and contemporary *activation*.

Imagination, motivation and activation make landscapes visible

First, the poem invites its readers to imagine an episode that could potentially take place in anyone's life. As the words meet the eyes of the reader, they support the realisation of an *image* perceived by the reading subject, however invisible for others. In order to be known to others and to become an object of discursive exchange, the image has to acquire a position in an intersubjective world. The materialisation of the image follows articulated *motifs*, such as the woods, the flute or the boy's wandering. These motifs in no way appear out of thin air or float in a void, even though they *could* be assembled out of all kinds of material things. Motifs are closely attached to a *horizon of motion*, reflecting the boy's roaming in the woods, and a *horizon of comprehension*, reflecting the boy's gradual acquisition of insight about his passionate experiences. From a wide range of opportunities, both the landscape image of the poet and the poem's objective motifs are attached to a piece of land and connected to an attitude to nature which has found expression in the pastoral tradition in Western culture. The act of imagination provided for by the analytical narrative is the essential aspect of a visual rationality, and is the foundation we must rely on when our goal is to raise landscape awareness. Imagination ties an individual's invisible image to visible motifs that are drawn from within the frames of shared horizons of motion and comprehension.

Second, the poem invites its readers to trace the image back to its *pastoral* sources. As the words meet the eyes of the reader, the image of a boy roaming in the woods *emerges into appearance*. With Ken Hiltner (Hiltner, 2011) we shall trace how landscapes emerge into appearance and why this appearance is not a matter of a day's habitual course, but emerges as a rare event. The boy is troubled by his longing for the melody he once perceived in the woods. He thereby enters a *liminal* state of mind, here expressed as the motivation to stop the flux of nature by making it into a replicable object of possession. With the art historian Erwin Panofsky (Panofsky, 1982) we shall trace pastoral landscapes' display of a discrepancy between opposite life forces that govern the human condition at any time. In the end, the boy's struggles with his passion to master the melody's presence open his eyes and his thoughts to an *emancipating* insight. With the literary scholar Paul Alpers (Alpers, 1996) we shall trace the pastoral way of dealing with life as the individual's reflection on his or her "strength relative to the world", and as a potentially emancipatory attitude. All these instances of motivation, *emergence into appearance*, *discrepancy* and *emancipation* sustain the reflective process in which landscape as *sight* is intrinsically bound to its meaning and evaluation, an *insight*.

Finally, the poem invites its readers to activate and actualise the image, referring it to what they are presently doing in their contemporary, everyday life. As the words meet the eyes of the reader, they symbolically depict the area as the world in which humanity moves, the things humanity fabricates, and lastly the stance humanity takes in relation to nature's variety and change. Arendt has described these practices as *labour*, *work* and *action*.

These practices are the fundamental conditions "under which life on earth has been given to man" (Arendt, 1998:7). As the boy unconsciously goes about his daily life (*labour*), roaming in the woods, the surroundings attract his attention in a way that is poetically visualised in the form of a wonderful but, alas, illusive melody. Once aware of it, he starts longing to relive his wonderful dream, and he sets about carving a flute (*work*) with which to bring the tune to life again and ensure its lasting presence. But the flute, he realises, cannot make it reappear as he first heard it. In the poetic shape of the voice of the Master (*action*), he admits that his work is a manifestation of human hubris and reconciles himself with that insight.

Landscapes as statements and ideas

The final voice, an *action* on the part of the poet, is a statement. It represents the insight that the tune will forever remain one of nature's secrets, one that humanity might sometimes come close to taking part in but will never be able to capture entirely. In Arendt's terminology, *action* holds a special position. It is the oral communication between individuals, the way in which the individual, through his or her utterances, takes a stand in the world and declares his or her singularly outstanding capacities. It is the *zoon politicon*'s characteristic way of expressing its unique potential as an individual of the human species: through articulating a *response* to its present environment. Through speech, the analyst constructs a temporary image of the world that is independent of direct involvement with the "'artificial' world of things" (*work*) or "the biological process of the human body": "Action, the only activity that goes on directly between men without the intermediary of things or matter, corresponds to the human condition of plurality, to the fact that men, not Man, live on the earth and inhabit the world" (Arendt, 1998:7).

Only in the *action* of the analyst can the different landscape shareholders that are gathered in dialogic imagination, pastoral motivation and current actualisation be linked. It is the *action* of the analyst, the articulation of a landscape, which foregrounds some images in favour of others and assembles them into visible material motifs of a currently relevant landscape. The *action* of the analyst, the Master's voice, links sensations to meaning within the frames of a lasting narrative. Any landscape analysed by an analyst is similarly reconfigured through the language and speech of the analyst. As we credit the poet for a poem, we should credit the landscape analyst for the landscape of the analysis.

Both the motivation to make land visible as landscape and the activation of images related to contemporary practices ensue from the performance of a landscape *idea* symbolising a humanity-nature relationship. An idea always guides the whole composition of an analytical narrative. Originally, "an idea or eidos is the shape or blueprint the craftsman must

have in front of his mind's eye before he begins his work" (Arendt, 1978:104)
Still linked to humanity as toolmaker (in the activity of *work*), the idea was
a material template, which the craftsperson used as his or her ideal before
and after the production of a thing. In the activity of *action*, however, as
in the case of the landscape analyst, this template must not be understood
as a model for exact replication, but as the *image* that he has "in front of
his mind's eye" before he starts his narration. The idea acts like the melody
in the poem. It is present although it cannot be mastered. It connects an
individual aesthetically and immediately to an area, although it cannot be
represented to others without speech and imaginative language. In this way,
the presence and impact of the melody in the poem resembles our idea of
landscape itself, human engagement with land.

Inherited and transformed landscapes

The picture *Seljefløiten* (*The Willow Flute*) by Christian Skredsvig, painted
130 years ago, shows a boy playing the flute by a brook at its outlet into
the lake Dælivannet. The site lies within the boundaries of a protected area
on the outskirts of the Oslo metropolitan area. At the site today, a signpost
directs visitors' attention so as to merge their perception of the presently
overgrown ditch, lake shore and far hillside with the features of the famous
painting (Figure 1.1). The act of imagination is helped in that the site itself
has been rearranged and is managed with reference to the picture. A bench
and table have been set up for us to sit and contemplate the serenity of
the lake and surrounding forested hills. We realise how the painting has
been used as a model for clearing wild brush and reconstructing the site
as a pastoral scene. Even as Skredsvig was still making the first sketches
for *Seljefløiten*, he was directly inspired by Bjørnson's poem *Tonen*. For
Skredsvig as for Bjørnson, as for the reconstruction team or even visitors to
the site at Dælivannet, the *landscape idea* acts according to the American
landscape photographer Ansel Adams' description of visualisation: "To
visualize an image [...] is to see it clearly in the mind prior to exposure, a
continuous projection from composing the image through the final print"
(Adams, 2003:ix).

The same preparatory function of the idea is recognised by the landscape architect James Corner when he points at how landscape architecture
derives "from an impulse to reshape large areas of land according to *prior
imaging*" (Corner, 1999:153). When thought of as an idea inherent in anything from a painted canvas, a printed page or a restored ditch, landscapes
are essentially more uniform than their medium of expression indicates. As
the cultural geographers Dennis Cosgrove and Stephen Daniels once stated,
"[a] landscape park is more palpable but no more real, nor less imaginary,
than a landscape painting or poem" (Cosgrove and Daniels, 1988:1). The
landscape that is so peacefully depicted in *Seljefløiten*, and in other paintings

by Skredsvig's colleagues and friends, is part of the most popular recreational area in the municipality of Bærum today. Visitors are attracted by what it has to offer in terms of experiences such as smooth forest paths, rocky climbs with great views, light reflections on water, birdsong and other animal sounds, the odours and atmospheres of the seasons etc. – all that nature has to offer and that compels the perceptive human *to see* the area as *landscape*. The painting itself as well as its status as protected landscape are part of this seeing, in so far as they are known to the visitors and thereby belong to their horizon of comprehension. Similarly, the area itself is part of the perception of the painting by visitors in the National Gallery in Oslo, in so far as it is known to the observers.

Figure 1.1 Christian Skredsvig's painting "The Boy with the Willow Flute", signposted at the picnic site by Dælivannet in Bærum municipality as visual reference.

In a mutual exchange and interplay between land and words, images and verbal articulations, the entire process of landscape formation is tied to the idea of landscape. Without that idea being shared, no communication would be possible, be it via a book page, a ditch or a canvas. When the reader reads the words on the signpost, when the rambler's feet touch the ground, when the visitor observes the characteristics of the land surface, these sensations are but brief glimpses reminding him or her of an overall idea that is stored in language and prevails as *landscape*. As the poem illustrates, landscapes are conceived in contemplative hindsight and uttered as fulfilled thoughts. They emerge when the process of perception and conception itself is reiterated in a narrative, which keeps in play the area seen as the habitat of an organic being (roaming in the woods/experiences), as the result of material work (making a flute/poem) and as the comprehension of an idea or insight (hearing the voice/inhabiting what the voice says). Any one of the three aspects of the poetic utterance depends on the fulfilment of the others for itself to make sense.

Landscape analysis as action reflecting on the human condition

The poem *Tonen* offers its readers an image by means of words. We have explained the presence of this image as a result of what we have called visual rationality: its presence in imagination, its motivation in the pastoral tradition, and its activation in a contemporary and innovative situation. The overall *performance* of the analytical narrative brings all these aspects of visual rationality together into a contemporary and visible landscape. Even though the physical layout of the land or its accessibility may change, as landscape the area is nevertheless still in reach of our memory and language, and thus negotiable through human *action*. The rearrangement and management of the site at Dælivannet is an example of such an *action*: a site's material layout is rearranged to provide a sight in accordance with a work of art.

Investigating landscape as utterances within memory and language represents an alternative to mapping the history or physical features of a site. Contrary to mapping the vegetation or building typology in a place, the meaning content of landscapes is not derived from features of the land, but appears as an outcome of the landscape analyst's interpretation, the *action* itself. The approach aims for what Panofsky has described as the "intrinsic meaning or content, constituting the world of 'symbolic' values" (Panofsky, 1972 :14). The analyst presents this meaning through his or her narrative, lending the interpretative momentum metonymically to a material and visible motif.

Thus, from the point of view of the landscape analyst, landscape changes are not primarily effectuated through transformations of the land's features, but through a switch in the type of vision which governs the perception. If we look at the poem as a whole in those terms, it is a testimony to how the transitions from *labour* to *work* to *action* involve a growing awareness through a process of reflection, which results in a presented and evaluated landscape and in the utterance of a potential insight and ethical ideal. Thus, in addition to determining the way land is conceptualised as symbolic land-scape, these changes in perspective, even more importantly, change the degree of understanding implied in "seeing". As the boy's *work* and *labour* are replaced by *action*, the material and organic landscapes are simultaneously replaced by a conceived and cognised landscape. Through his engagement with land, his imagination is stimulated and his horizon of comprehension similarly expanded.

Arcadia updated directs its attention especially towards landscape analysis as a narrative device for raising landscape awareness. As in the poem, both the initial and concluding events of perception must be called forth through a language with which the individual expert hopes to engage the reader in an aesthetic act of creative criticism. In their dedication to an ever-evolving world, landscape analyses thereby act as reflections on the human condi-tion displayed in the humanity-nature relationship: "Reflection or reflective thought is the ability of man to single out from the whole undiscriminated mass of the stream of floating sensuous phenomena certain fixed elements in order to isolate them and to concentrate attention upon them" (Cassirer, 1944:39–40). A "holistic", created phenomenon such as *landscape* (Herlin, 2004; Kaplan, 2009; Antrop and Van Eetvelde, 2018) can only be sustained through a dialogue between the many, when engaged in a shared idea, as a kind of co-creation (Benjamin, 1991:443; Gadamer, 2010:150; Rancière, 2009; Butler and Åkerskog, 2014; Stenseke, 2016; Dalglish and Leslie, 2016). Thus, the *performance* of the analytical narrative represents an ever-present opportunity to gain awareness of society's ways of "ordering meaning and value that clarifies our situation today" (Marx, 2000:4). Landscape analysis provides an opportunity to give contemporary human liminality a visible shape through the medium of land.

Activating and actualising the landscape ideal of the *insider*

Unlike 130 years ago when Skredsvig's painting was created, the area around Dælivannet today has legal status as "protected cultural land-scape" (Miljøverndepartementet, 1978). The documents which provide the arguments for protecting the area against any activity that might result in a change of the area's "type or character" (Miljøverndepartementet, 1978:3) are typical of how landscapes have come to be approached in planning. They list landscape qualities such as beauty, dramatic terrain, interesting geo-logical features, diverse vegetation, and actively farmed pastures, fields and forest. They highlight the area's great historical depth, manifested through ancient relics, as well as its importance as a location in Norwegian art history, the earlier artists' colony there, of which Skredsvig was a member, having contributed to the "appreciation of landscape beauty in Norway" (Miljødirektoratet, 2018). The protected area also includes four nature reserves, and rare flora and fauna as well as geological and archaeological elements are documented through the respective scientific terminologies. What in Bjørnson's poem is a human idea of Nature has become nature *tout court*. Whereas in Enlightenment and Romantic thinking landscapes still had meaning as *ways of imagining* the land with various religious, philosophical or political if not utopian symbolic connotations, landscape has now regressed into *land*. The melody is being mistaken for the flute or the woods.

In recent years, especially after the coming into force of the European Landscape Convention, which posits *landscape* as "an area, as perceived by people", criticism has increasingly been voiced within landscape planning against the most common landscape analysis methods (Brunetta and Voghera, 2008; Fiskevold, 2013, 2012, 2011; Geelmuyden and Fiskevold, 2016; Geelmuyden, 2016; Butler, 2014; Stephenson, 2008; Dakin, 2003; Jørgensen et al., 2016; Olwig et al., 2016). Nevertheless, landscape analysis and evaluation methods described in recent publications (Stahlschmidt et al., 2017) lean on a modernist positivistic approach to landscapes, that is, still understand them as material entities, or as physical stimuli to which humans react. Although this approach is useful within its defined limits, it seems that the critical, reflective aspect of landscape, its legacy from the pastoral tradition implied in the European Landscape Convention, has been overlooked and neglected. This is remarkable, since throughout scholarly landscape studies, particularly in cultural geography and anthropology, a different outlook on the concept of landscape has been voiced for more than 30 years (Doherty and Waldheim, 2016; Trepl, 2012; Schmeling and Schmitz-Emans, 2007; Groh and Groh, 1991; Cosgrove, 1998; Ritter, 1974). John Wylie (Wylie, 2007) has labelled this development "the cultural turn" in landscape studies because landscapes here are seen primarily as cultural constructions. This critical scholarly debate has stayed far removed from the practices of planners and architects and from public decision-making processes.

Against the currently prevailing professional methodology, we argue that the landscape analyst must refrain from mere reproduction of known images and concepts, and seek new ways of symbolising the humanity-nature relationship that address today's burning issues. On the other hand, against Denis Cosgrove's call for a "critical, socially conscious, outsider's perspective" (Cosgrove, 1998:xi), we argue that a critical outsider's perspective on landscape is hardly possible: any understanding of landscape in *planning* must depart from a language in which it can be presented as a shared or shareable vision of the outside world. In *Arcadia updated* we shall extend and make explicit the influence of the pastoral heritage on contemporary planning. We will do this from the expert point of view, elaborating on the potentials inherent in the vision of *insiders to the pastoral landscape tradition* for a future practice of landscape analysis.

In the following chapters, we will discuss the challenge of analysing landscapes as well as demonstrate a new analytical approach. We shall trace the analytical narrative as *work* and *action* from its sources in the pastoral tradition (chapter two), through its historical manifestations in Western society (chapter three), to some recent attempts to implement it within the confines of conventional landscape analysis methods (chapter four), as well as to examples of its potential as images emphasising humans' engagement with land as either organic, material or articulated (chapter five), and finally, to its possible future role as a tool for planning in an increasingly digitised society (chapter six).

References

Adams, A. 2003. *The camera*, New York, Little, Brown and Co.

Alpers, P. 1996. *What is pastoral?* Chicago, University of Chicago Press.

Andrews, M. 1999. *Landscape and Western art*, Oxford, Oxford University Press.

Antrop, M. & Van Eetvelde, V. 2018. *Landscape perspectives: the holistic nature of landscape*, Dordrecht, Springer.

Arendt, H. 1978. *The life of the mind*, San Diego, Harcourt.

Arendt, H. 1998. *The human condition*, Chicago, University of Chicago Press.

Benjamin, W. 1991. *Gesammelte Schriften*, Frankfurt am Main, Suhrkamp.

Bjørnson, B. 1915. *Poems and songs*, New York, American Scandinavian Foundation.

Brunetta, G. & Voghera, A. 2008. Evaluating landscape for shared values: tools, principles, and methods. *Landscape Research*, 33, 71–87.

Butler, A. 2014. *Developing theory of public involvement in landscape planning*, Uppsala, Swedish University of Agricultural Sciences.

Butler, A. & Åkerskog, A. 2014. Awareness-raising of landscape in practice: an analysis of Landscape Character Assessments in England. *Land Use Policy*, 36, 441–449.

Cassirer, E. 1944. *An essay on man: an introduction to a philosophy of human culture*, New Haven, Yale University Press.

Corner, J. 1999. *Eidetic operations and new landscapes*, New York, Princeton Architectural Press.

Cosgrove, D. 1998. *Social formation and symbolic landscape*, Madison, University of Wisconsin Press.

Cosgrove, D. & Daniels, S. 1988. *The iconography of landscape: essays on the symbolic representation, design and use of past environments*, Cambridge, Cambridge University Press.

Council of europe. 2000. *European Landscape Convention*. Strasbourg, Council of Europe.

Dakin, S. 2003. There's more to landscape than meets the eye: towards inclusive landscape assessment in resource and environmental management. *The Canadian Geographer*, 47, 185–200.

Dalglish, C. & Leslie, A. 2016. A question of what matters: landscape characterisation as a process of situated, problem-orientated public discourse. *Landscape Research*, 2, 1–15.

Doherty, G. & Waldheim, C. 2016. Is landscape...? Essays on the identity of landscape, New York, Routledge.

Fiskevold, M. 2011. *Veien som vilje og forestilling: analysemetoder for landskap og estetisk erfaring*, Ås, Universitetet for miljø- og biovitenskap.

Fiskevold, M. 2012. Landskap på avveie? Landskapsanalysen som veiviser i en pluralistisk samtid. *Arkitektur N*, 8, 12–19.

Fiskevold, M. 2013. *The ELC's call for expert landscape identification: conceptual challenges*, Florence, Uniscape.

Gadamer, H.-G. 2010. *Sannhet og metode: grunntrekk i en filosofisk hermeneutikk*, Oslo, Bokklubben.

Geelmuyden, A. K. 1989a. *Landskapsopplevelse og landskap: ideologi eller ideologikritikk? Et essay om de teoretiske vilkårene for vurdering av landskap i arealplanleggingen*, Ås, Institutt for landskapsarkitektur.

Geelmuyden, A. K. 1989b. Økologisk arkitektur: en byggekultur på leting etter naturen – men hvilken natur? *Byggekunst*, 89, 237–242.

Geelmuyden, A. K. 1993. Landskapsanalyse: planredskap og erkjennelsesvei. *Byggekunst*, 93, 152–157.

Geelmuyden, A. K. 2016. Landscape assessments in imaginative (poetic) landscape narratives: contemporary pastorals. *In:* Jørgensen, K., Clemetsen, M., Thorén, K. H. & Richardson, T. (eds) *Mainstreaming landscape through the European Landscape Convention*. Oxford: Routledge.

Geelmuyden, A. K. & Fiskevold, M. 2016. Den europeiske landskapskonvensjonen: en pastorale for vår egen tid? *Nordisk Arkitekturforskning*, 28, 51–79.

Groh, R. & Groh, D. 1991. *Weltbild und Naturaneignung: zur Kulturgeschichte der Natur*, Frankfurt am Main, Suhrkamp.

Herlin, I. S. 2004. New challenges in the field of spatial planning: landscapes. *Landscape Research*, 29, 399–411.

Hiltner, K. 2011. *What else is pastoral? Renaissance literature and the environment*, Ithaca, Cornell University Press.

Hunt, J. D. 1992. *The pastoral landscape*, Washington, DC, National Gallery of Art.

Hunt, J. D. 2000. *Greater perfections: the practice of garden theory*, London, Thames & Hudson.

Jones, M. 2007. The European Landscape Convention and the question of public participation. *Landscape Research*, 32, 613–633.

Jones, M., Jones, M. & Stenseke, M. 2011. *The European Landscape Convention: challenges of participation*, Dordrecht, Springer.

Jørgensen, K., Clemetsen, M., Thorén, K. H. & Richardson, T. 2016. *Mainstreaming landscape through the European Landscape Convention*, Abingdon, Routledge.

Kaplan, A. 2009. Landscape architecture's commitment to landscape concept: a missing link? *JoLA – Journal on Landscape Architecture*, 4(1), 56–65.

Lyotard, J.-F. 1984. *The postmodern condition: a report on knowledge*, Manchester, Manchester University Press.

Marx, L. 2000. *The machine in the garden: technology and the pastoral ideal in America*, Oxford, Oxford University Press.

Miljødirektoratet. 2018. *Kolsås/Dælivann* [Online]. Available at: faktaark.naturbase. no/Vern?id=VV00001820 [Accessed 3 March 2018].

Miljøverndepartementet. 1978. Forskrift om vern av Kolsås-Dælivann landskapsvernområde med plante- og fuglelivsfredninger og fire naturreservater i Bærum kommune, Akershus. *In*: Miljøverndepartementet (ed.) *FOR-1978-06-30-2*, Oslo, Miljøverndepartementet.

Olwig, K. 1996. Recovering the substantive nature of landscape. *Annals of the Association of American Geographers*, 86(4), 630–653.

Olwig, K. R., Dalglish, C., Fairclough, G. & Herring, P. 2016. Introduction to a special issue: the future of landscape characterisation, and the future character of landscape – between space, time, history, place and nature. *Landscape Research*, 2, 1–6.

Panofsky, E. 1972. *Studies in iconology: humanistic themes in the art of the Renaissance*, New York, Icon Editions.

Panofsky, E. 1982. *Meaning in the visual arts*, Chicago, University of Chicago Press.

Rancière, J. 2009. *The emancipated spectator*, London, Verso Books.

Ritter, J. 1974. *Subjektivität: sechs Aufsätze*, Frankfurt, Suhrkamp.

Ruff, A. R. 2015. *Arcadian visions: pastoral influences on poetry, painting and the design of landscape*, Oxford, Windgather Press.

Schmeling, M. & Schmitz-Emans, M. (eds). 2007. *Das Paradigma der Landschaft in Moderne und Postmoderne*, Würzburg, Königshausen & Neumann.

Stahlschmidt, P., Swaffield, S., Primdahl, J. & Nellemann, V. 2017. *Landscape analysis: investigating the potentials of space and place*, Abingdon, Routledge.

Stenseke, M. 2016. Integrated landscape management and the complicating issue of temporality. *Landscape Research*, 2, 1–13.

Stephenson, J. 2008. The cultural values model: an integrated approach to values in landscapes. *Landscape and Urban Planning*, 84, 127–139.

Trepl, L. 2012. *Die Idee der Landschaft: eine Kulturgeschichte von der Aufklärung bis zur Ökologiebewegung*, Bielefeld, Transcript.

Weller, R. 2006. An art of instrumentality: thinking through landscape urbanism. *In*: Waldheim, C. (ed.) *The landscape urbanism reader*, New York, Princeton Architectural Press.

Williams, R. 1993. *The country and the city*, London, Hogarth Press.

Wylie, J. 2007. *Landscape*, London, Routledge.

Chapter 2

The pastoral tradition as inherited motives

Pastoral attitude and visual rationality

As we see in the case of *Seljefløiten*, the pastoral tradition spans generations, and as individual utterances has found expression through very different means in history. The words of Bjørnson's poem, the colours of Skredsvig's painting, the design of the site at Dælivannet and the cultural discourses concerning it are all aspects of the narrative which has shaped and is still shaping the landscape of Dælivannet. In the *actions* of both an expert author and an eventual reader, a landscape analysis appears as a materialised *work*. The entirely invisible acts of writing by Bjørnson or painting by Skredsvig produced the objectively visible *motifs* in the poem and painting. When uttered, a landscape is always aimed at an expected but not yet articulated response. It is a re-collection, an act of assembling a temporary image in a lasting motif within the accidentally present horizon. In the plethora of human perception's never-ending lapses from order into chaos and vice versa, the appearance of a motif into visibility is a landscape's lifejacket, rescuing it from either solipsism or objectivism, from mere idle talk or ana-chronistic conventionalism. As a matter of fact, the tradition of pastoral landscape vision can be regarded as a passion for visibility.

A pastoral landscape articulates a visual exchange between humanity and land, and reveals a rational human way of dealing with the environment. An *analytical* landscape narrative may help us to understand in what way the different layers and networks of meaning contribute to both the percep-tion and the understanding of a place. The pastoral attitude can be traced back to artistic fields as different as literature, figurative art and garden art. In addition to these materialisations of the tradition, the scholarly world has produced a wide range of interpretations of the various artworks. The joint efforts of artistic imaging and scholarly critique have provided a rich array of sources for a continuous reproduction of meaning and a continu-ation of the tradition itself. In this chapter we shall point to some aspects of the visual rationale of the tradition and show how these constitute a set of *pastoral motives*. The culture of *pastoral landscape vision* places substantial faith in the *emergence into appearance* of a landscape being shared, in an enlightening *discrepancy* that conditions its utterance, and lastly in the subjective *emancipatory* potential it offers to the aware individual. Together, these landscape pastoral motives constitute a kind of rationality, which takes its point of departure in the visual whole of a landscape.

Shared appearances: the constructive act of seeing

The dialogue between Tityrus and Meliboeus in the first of Vergil's ten *Eclogues* is a frequently quoted episode in the pastoral scholarly tradition (Alpers, 1996; Marx, 2000; Hiltner, 2011). In one of the passages from this dialogue (1, 36–39), where the exiled shepherd Meliboeus meets his old friend Tityrus, Meliboeus' gestures and words indicate that even the fountains and orchards have been calling for Tityrus' attention (Leach, 1974:123):

> I wondered, Amaryllis, why you so sadly called on the gods, and for whom you left your apples hanging neglected on the tree. Tityrus was away from here. The very pine trees were calling you, Tityrus. The fountains and the orchards were calling after you.

Meliboeus repeatedly tries to draw Tityrus' attention to the state of the land by pointing at visible features such as apples and pine trees, a *motif* in this *Eclogue*. The material things and qualities which look so appealing to Meliboeus are, however, less noticed by the actual keeper of the land, Tityrus. Tityrus is of a very different mindset, enjoying his newly won status as a released slave. He wards off all of the visual sketches laid out in Meliboeus' speech, unintentionally demonstrating an attitude that the American literary scholar Ken Hiltner characterises as "like that of an audience member (spectator) so obsessed with the human action on stage that the scenery is completely ignored, even though something altogether extraordinary is happening there" (Hiltner, 2011:39).

Visual attention: the event of seeing

An ignorance of landscape, or the refusal to perform a constructive seeing act, is the condition from which any visual attention has to be created and will depart. Whether we as readers catch sight of Tityrus' orchard or the land enters our thoughts as the lost homeland of the exiled Meliboeus, we understand that the perception of a motif and its realisation as an image of our own always disrupts the flux of *labour* and forces the individual to take a stance in the world, an *action*. The interruption of absent-mindedness may happen anywhere, affect anyone and be set into action more or less frequently. The observation of the berries disrupts Meliboeus'

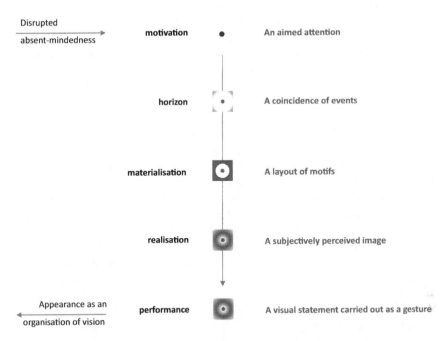

Figure 2.1 The symbolic event of seeing traced from the moment of attention to the area down to a gesturing landscape utterance.

thoughts of his exile and gives them an immediate form, shape and location. Simultaneously, his verbal and gestural utterance punctuates his ongoing scanning of the land, incorporating the sight of the berries into a motif of abundance and waste, which in turn illuminates the reality of his exile. Disrupted absent-mindedness is the usual event that causes a motif's *emergence into appearance* (Hiltner, 2011:39). What is extraordinary in the display of this episode is thus not only what is going on in the scenery (the wastefulness), but the fact that the images and their corresponding motifs come into being at all (Figure 2.1).

Horizon: encircled by a potentially shared world

The dialogue between Meliboeus and Tityrus is an age-old testimony to how human vision captures or ignores aspects of the environment. Simultaneously, it tells a story of how humans throughout history have failed or succeeded in visualising their everyday surroundings as visible versions of their own actions, practices and life conditions. As the dialogue between Meliboeus and Tityrus shows, the features of the land that Meliboeus highlights as motifs are not perceived by Tityrus. Where

Meliboeus sees an agrarian dream, Tityrus keeps his vision well beyond the boundaries of his territory, instead orienting himself in relation to the distant seat of power, Rome. As the dialogue demonstrates in such an exemplary way, both the subjective perception of an image and its articulation as a motif in an objective medium (e.g. speech) owe their presence to an expectation. As former shepherds, both Meliboeus and Tityrus are qualified land watchers. They both have acquired experience through their work and dependence on the land. Standing in the orchard, they are both encircled by the same earthly horizon, but as their conversation proceeds, it becomes evident that their horizons of comprehension, as evoked by their respective life stories, are no longer congruent. This discrepancy of vision does not emerge into appearance until Meliboeus makes his image known through an utterance. It is only at the moment when Meliboeus transforms his view into an utterance that frames an image of his situation and articulates his perception in words that his vision is fulfilled and can be presented as a potentially communal event.

The motif, which *is* the visible outcome of a landscape utterance, *functions* as a symbol that infuses materiality with meaning. The unpicked fruit, which is the motif of Meliboeus' speech, functions as a symbol of his state of exile as well as his previous life and land, both of which he has been forced to leave. Actually, Meliboeus sees the land in a way that merges his life narrative with his visual sensation of colours and greyscales on site. The meaning which is attached to the land is not added later, but is part of the perception itself. By claiming that "[a] symbol has no actual existence as a part of the physical world; it has a 'meaning'" (Cassirer, 1944:57), Ernst Cassirer highlights the symbol's role both within a horizon of comprehension and as a constituent of human communication. Although symbolic images have no actual existence in the non-human world, they still heavily influence the human reception of that world. They carry with them a kind of pre-shaped meaning, an expectation of what is to be seen. The once shared experience that is now a lost common horizon of comprehension also lies at the heart of Meliboeus' frustration. He knows that Tityrus once shared his idealising views. Meliboeus is well aware that it is neither the friend's neglected harvest nor Tityrus' ignorance of the reason for his own perception of the orchard which upsets him. Rather, his dissatisfaction is grounded in the fact that Tityrus' attention is now governed by another collective way of seeing (normative horizon). In *that* symbolic image and visual culture, Meliboeus has no share.

Materialisation: the articulation of a visible motif

The materiality of apples, pine trees and fountains must of course be accepted as matters of fact that are independent of any human perception. However, their noted appearance, both as conventionally classified objects and more specifically as pastoral motifs, cannot be conceived independently of human activity and thought. Accepting the fact of Meliboeus' and Tityrus' two sights, we have to renounce any insistence on the *factual* existence of a landscape. The motif always appears as an object of perception, not as a material thing. As both part and product of the perceptive act, the meaning of the motif arises from *selection and arrangement*. Through the choice of words alone, the articulation of the scene between Meliboeus and Tityrus recounts a limited and definite version of an infinitude of possible experiences.

Pine trees, orchards and fountains were the elements calling for visual attention when Vergil worked on his *Eclogues*. Today, there are many other elements that call out for our attention and for a chance to emerge into appearance. In order to keep its relevance, the pastoral tradition has incessantly changed the material configuration of its motifs. Emerging motifs are as varied as human culture. Equally, the drive to ensure the relevance of pastoral motifs is as old as Vergil's accounts. "Virgil is not looking back to some sort of golden age, but rather to an historically situated, contemporary moment when the environment becomes the subject of thematic awareness at the very moment of its withdrawal" (Hiltner, 2011:37). The rearrangement of the motif in order to make it relevant is not only something that happens by coincidence, but must also be regarded as a characteristic trait of the pastoral attitude as such. Even Vergil broke from inherited pastoral convention, as the literary scholar Eleanor Winsor Leach points out (Leach, 1974:113):

> For Vergil, the departure from Theocritus is not a loss, but a rejection. Familiar Theocritean images of pastoral leisure and simplicity have become an illusionary vision that must be supplanted by images more vital and more representative of the contemporary world.

Thus, pastoral vision is always shaping and visualising contemporary events into showable motifs. As Hiltner repeatedly stresses, "[a]ny discussion of pastoral literature that does not explore how the figurative impacts the literal is simply incomplete" (Hiltner, 2011:40). Consequently, the motif emerges into appearance and becomes visible as an outcome of the will to make the contemporary world visible as it *is*. The pastoral attitude takes its stance at the core of contemporary successes or failures and trivialities. The coincidental appearance of a motif and the undetermined perception of an image have formed a creative basis for the invention of visual scenes since the Vergilian pastorals. In Winsor Leach's words (Leach, 1974:113):

> The variety of nature is the basis for the complexities of the *Eclogues*. The poems have no consistent landscape. No one image stands out as typically pastoral. Their world is created as microcosm of nature, offering the contrast that nature offers the eye.

A motif being an accidental appearance of a fragment of land implies, firstly, that its layout is coincidental, and secondly, that its potential for emerging into appearance is unlimited. Leo Marx recognises these tendencies in the development of American society. His conclusion is that "[t]he American case illustrates the extraordinary resilience of pastoralism – its capacity for adaptation to new times, new places, new social and political situations" (Marx, 1992:213). In the dialogue between Meliboeus and Tityrus, this dependency between the *conception* of the natural world on the one hand and its materiality on the other is clearly articulated. The sight of a lost harvest, which entirely fills Meliboeus' image, signals the presence of *his* meaningful position and perspective. As the scene demonstrates, the resilience of the motif is based upon a motivation by the creator of the image, in this case Meliboeus as well as Vergil, to make the contemporary world visible.

Realisation: a subjectively perceived image

The pastoral tradition is a tradition of negotiated contradictions. The permanence (as *work*) and temporariness (as *action*) of the motif are but two versions of its fragility. As the motif itself evolves over time, the human motivation to mirror life conditions in visible configurations seems to prevail. However well articulated and well described a motif may be, the analytical narrative which effectuates its realisation requires an act of subjective imagination. The availability of the motif, its emergence into appearance, firstly requires the attention and willingness to see. Something's visibility is just one aspect of its being comprehended as a motif. Tityrus, according to Hiltner, shows no signs of such an attitude. Instead, his response to Meliboeus' site descriptions bears every sign of indifference and blindness. The realisation of the landscape utterance can only take place when, in a sharing of the utterance's horizon of comprehension, a visible motif can be incorporated into the imaginative realm of an individual. Without such subjective engagement, there is no landscape to see.

Tityrus fails to follow Meliboeus' sight. Although they are standing on the same spot at the same time, their vision of the land differs fundamentally. In different ways, their ability to see depends on a separation and distance from the place. Neither Tityrus nor Meliboeus have been able to carry on with their familiar lives. Both have had to change their ways due to changes in society. Tityrus has managed to adapt himself to the new civic order, while Meliboeus has been forced to leave his much beloved homeland. This separation has respectively brought the two further away from and closer to the ability to image the land as landscape. Tityrus' concern is his role as a free man, and he shows no interest in the nearby land. Meliboeus', on the other hand, with the motif of the unpicked fruit, simultaneously calls forth the events of his former life *and* the potential for that way of life which presents itself in the disused orchard of his former companion. A former, once habitual experience is transformed into an observable and comprehensible object of regret *and* imagination. The presence of the perceiver's pastoral landscape image is always a kind of *rebirth,* a term used by Cassirer to explain any process of image formation (Cassirer, 1944:51):

> In man we cannot describe recollection as a simple return of an event, as a faint image or copy of former impressions. It is not simply a repetition but rather a rebirth of the past; it implies a creative and constructive process. It is not enough to pick up isolated data of our past experience; we must really *re-collect* them, we must organize and synthesize them, and assemble them into a focus of thought.

In that an awareness of land as landscape is uttered, what motivated it is already a moment in the past. The act of imagination requires a distance from the complexity of the remembered area, but at the same time a proximity to the distinct and singular things that can become reminders and referents. The image of the scene appears as a reconstruction of a continuum of ongoing events of experience and reflection. It is the image that an attentive and motivated observer perceives as an instant achievement, which soon after will be replaced by another fresh impression.

Enlightening discrepancy: the dialectic act of seeing

As a little scene from Vergil's third *Eclogue* indicates (3, 98–99), the diversity in the appearance of pastoral motifs is a product of a tension between existential pleasures and anxieties in human life (Leach, 1974:179): "You boys who gather flowers and berries born from the earth, get away from here, O boys; a cold snake hides in the grass." Pastoral episodes enact the way humans are drawn between their desires and the forces that obstruct the realisation of those desires. The pastoral mode and its visual outcomes are constantly influenced by a dialectic between positive and negative ideals. The tempting sight of the flowers and berries changes with the knowledge of the snake hiding in the grass. The colours of flowers and berries might visually remind us of their beauty and delicious taste, but only insofar as we are unaware of the snake.

Horizon: dialectical seeing

In the pastoral tradition, we have to search for the symbolic meaning of motifs by way of a detour into a negative ideal which provides a productively contrasting foil for them. In the pastoral tradition, contrasting forces provide an imagery of *liminal* landscapes allowing us to visually *explore* the world. One of the famous essays describing this pastoral discrepancy is Panofsky's examination of the two versions of *Et in Arcadia ego,* two paintings by the French artist Nicolas Poussin. The Louvre version

Figure 2.2 Poussin, *Et in Arcadia ego,* first (Chatsworth) version.

(Figure 2.3) depicts a group of shepherds arranged around a tomb in the middle of a forest environment. Panofsky describes the scene as an event of reflective hindsight and dialogue: "Instead of being checked in their progress by an unexpected and terrifying phenomenon, they are absorbed in calm discussion and pensive contemplation" (Panofsky, 1982:313). The whole group is engaged in the contemplation of the tomb and in reading the letters on it that spell *Et in Arcadia ego*. In Panofsky's translation, this inscription, which commands the shepherds' attention and silences their songs, means "Even in Arcadia, I, Death, hold sway" (Panofsky, 1982:310). With the introduction of the concept "death" in the tangible environment of "life", the pastoral landscape motif is made part of both the positive and the

Figure 2.3 Poussin, *Et in Arcadia ego*, second (Louvre) version.

negative idealities of human life, "a present happiness menaced by death" (Panofsky, 1982:296). In this way, the pastoral landscape image includes both the ideals of life and creation on the one hand, and death and dissolution on the other. The duality of the pastoral episode reflects its true engagement with the course of human life. The visual exploration of the painting must be equally directed at the creative efforts of humanity and the destructive forces of nature. A reading of the *Eclogues*, for example, reveals that there are almost more snakes than flowers and berries in the different motifs which bear the text. The life of the shepherds is by no means as happy as many of their depictions seem to suggest. Winsor Leach, who frequently mentions the "frustrated shepherd", contends that the pastoral world consists of both sweetness and imperfections: "In fact, the imaginary worlds of pastoral exist at a midpoint between the ideals of myth and the realities of physical nature" (Leach, 1974:70). The positive and negative ideals of the pastoral episode mutually criticise and reinforce one another. For the shepherds as well as for ordinary people, the concept of death may symbolise a state of absolute dissolution but also a rebirth, a new kind of presence. Interpreted as concept, death might be understood literally as the end of life-sustaining *labour*. On the other hand, death could be associated with the completion of the *process* of fabrication (*work*), or it may be seen as the closing of the *process* of discursive imagining (*action*). Awareness of abruption and death becomes the necessary fixed point which opposes the developments and movements of life. The painting by Poussin depicts just such a transition between opposing ideal states. In Marx's metaphorical design, death – in the industrialised society version – acts as a counterforce, a parergon, bringing a world "which is more 'real' into juxtaposition with an idyllic version" (Marx, 2000:25). In this metaphor, both the driving forces and the counterforces have their function and relevance as "[t]hey illuminate each other" (Marx, 2000:30).

Materialised motifs show the interdependency of positive and negative ideals

The reciprocal interdependency of the positive and negative ideals points to different versions of human engagement and partaking in the land. When these ideals are materialised and given visibility as motifs – say, flowers and berries, or snake and tomb – they simultaneously make explicit both driving forces and counterforces. As the episode with the shepherds and the tomb clearly demonstrates, pastoral motifs depend on different types of discrepancy found in the human adaptation to challenges in the land. Winsor Leach operates with four different modes of pastoral landscapes. She connects "the *farm* with man's desire for order, the *rustic world* with human anxieties and uncertainties, the *wilderness* with uncontrolled passions, and the *locus amoenus* with man's fantasies and desire for withdrawal" (Leach, 1974:112). Winsor Leach treats her modes of landscape as ideals that positively bring forth visible motifs whenever they are practised on a piece of land. She emphasises that "[t]he four modes of landscapes in the poems have associations with patterns of conduct and thought" (Leach, 1974:112). Their motifs will differ in their layout, although their motivation may outlive nations, cultures and eras.

Another literary scholar, Timothy Saunders, similarly observes that the poetic use and significance of land confiscation in Vergil's first *Eclogue* and in Roman society makes this encroachment a part of the pastoral utterance (Saunders, 2008:92). Hiltner's environmentalist approach to pastoral works accordingly highlights the consequences of urban sprawl in 16th-century England and how "the endangered countryside began to appear as if for the first time to its citizens and artists" (Hiltner, 2011:6). The dialectic between social power structures and the life conditions of the individual is equally evident in Winsor Leach's interpretations, but in contrast to Hiltner, she puts the emphasis on the share of the individual's approach in the meaning of the poems. The materialisation of human life's discrepancies into visible motifs forces pastoral characters "to understand that their countryside belongs within the framework of the great world" (Leach, 1974:79–80). In pastoral presentations, human engagement with land resides in individual imagination.

Realisation: developing a subjective imagery based on worldly tensions

The montage of oppositions which is objectively displayed in a pastoral utterance is simultaneously subjectively apprehended and synthesised by a reader of a document or a listener to a speech. A subjectively apprehended image is a collection of motifs materialising from a changing and diverse world of impressions. Cassirer sees this synthesising aspect of imagination as the work of symbolic memory, "the process by which man not only repeats his past experience but also reconstructs this experience. Imagination becomes a necessary element of true recollection" (Cassirer, 1944:52). The imaginative exploration of land as landscape links the past to the future, experiences to hopes, sense impressions to reflective thought. The image of the cold snake in Vergil's third *Eclogue* is not that of a reptile on a blank sheet. Rather, it emerges into appearance as image and motif partly due to the events in the text, partly due to individual experience and partly as inherited convention. Eventually, individual experience will create a register of imageries, however full of contrasts and disruptions rather than harmony and completeness. On the other hand, this collection of diverse images and their concurring motifs can be enriched and renewed as it enters into the inscrutable ways of visual exploration.

The relation between positive and negative idealities is what may fuel a visual exploration of pastoral episodes and thus constitutes the fundamental dynamism of pastoral imaging and narration. As is apparent in the montage of the berries and the snake in Vergil's third *Eclogue* as well as in Panofsky's essay on *Et in Arcadia ego*, the tension between the postulated, positive ideal and the experienced, negative ideal plays a crucial role in keeping this episodic dynamism vital and relevant (Panofsky, 1982:300):

> It was then, in the imagination of Virgil, and Virgil alone, that the concept of Arcady, as we know it, was born – that a bleak and chilly district of Greece came to be transfigured into an imaginary realm of perfect bliss. But no sooner had this new, Utopian Arcady come into being than a discrepancy was felt between the supernatural perfection of an imaginary environment and the natural limitations of human life as it is.

The whole act of painting a harsh piece of land with sweetly flowering words is in itself an excellent way to demonstrate the influence of the latter over the former. But it is also an example of how worlds of imagination shed light on essential aspects of human life. Keeping moments poetically potent, and thus revelatory, requires the skill to explore the whole contemporary field of action and synthesise the offered sights into coherent landscape images. As Winsor Leach remarks, "[c]oherence cannot be inherited, but with each new venture into pastoral fiction it must be created anew"

(Leach, 1974:70). Whether the pastoral utterance has literary or political ambitions, its arguments must be fresh and relevant.

As the historical transformations of Arcadia in poetry demonstrate, once the different ideals of human engagement with land have found a home in humanity's symbolic imagination, previous perceptions of the world tend to be turned upside down. Cherished perspectives and well-known motifs themselves are transformed into a counterforce, thus threatening to neutralise the tension and liminal dynamism of pastorals. In late 19th-century American art, the train, for example, having been a negative ideal (i.e. machine as a counterforce to the positive ideal of the American landscape pastoral), eventually became incorporated into the idealising pastoral motif itself. "Now pastoralism was embodied in fresh, New World images of an ideal liminality, a potential harmony between society and nature" (Marx, 1992:213). *Outdated* products of modern infrastructure were now painted into the potential harmony between society and nature and seen against society's newer machineries. Only when a motif is capable of triggering subjective imagination by addressing some element's liminal societal status can its symbolic pastoral meaning be kept alive.

Subjective emancipation: the revelatory act of seeing

Horizon: visual evaluation – a motif's endurance as symbolic statement

A simple comparison, such as for instance the one made between the effect of a song and a rest in the grass or the quenching of thirst in the following quotation, shows how the juxtaposition of horizons may reveal a new perspective on the world (Leach, 1974:195): "Such is your song to me, godlike poet, as sleep in the grass to worn-out men; such a solace as the sweet waters in the leaping river give to thirst in summer heat" (*Eclogue* 5, 45–47). In Winsor Leach's words, "the more complex forms of pastoral do not embody a glorification but rather a critical evaluation of the pastoral dream" (Leach, 1974:36). Neither shifting appearances nor the evolving imagery of pastoral landscapes are neutral events in relation to a perceiving subject, a traditional way of living or the politics of a society. On the contrary, seen motifs and their articulation in images are deeply embedded in human life and conduct. But for pastoral landscape motifs to be symbolically potent, they must be subject to day-to-day evaluation and made relevant to problem-solving in an everyday, contemporary world. Only by rejecting one-sidedly idealising images and conventions – that is, given answers to how humans *should* relate to the world – can pastoral landscape appreciation reveal negative aspects of one's state of being and become a potential source of emancipation. The emergence into appearance of images and the articulation of contemporarily potent motifs require critical evaluation and determination.

As evident in the excerpt from the *Eclogues* above, visually evaluating a piece of land means using one's experience to compare between both positive and negative ideals, bringing them together in an individual horizon of comprehension.

In his much cited and referenced work *What is pastoral* (Alpers, 1996), Alpers ascribes much of the meaning of the literary pastoral tradition to the struggles of human life, rather than primarily to the humanity-nature relationship. Alpers thus tends to emphasise the life of the shepherds in favour of the environment in which this life takes place. Though much criticised by authors such as Hiltner for reducing the pastoral to political issues, Alpers does admit the relevance of the pastoral landscapes as long as "they are conceived as fit habitations for herdsmen or their equivalents" (Alpers, 1996:28). In fact, this is a more overt recognition of the relevance of landscapes in pastoral culture than it may at first seem. Through his interpretation of the impact of nature from the perspective of the herdsmen, Alpers draws attention to landscape as a clear act of symbolic image formation. Alpers' much repeated phrase "strength relative to the world" penetrates the diverse texts and sources he claims as representative of the pastoral mode and thereby part of the pastoral tradition: "The figure of the shepherd is felt to be representative precisely in figuring every or any man's strength relative to the world" (Alpers, 1996:50). By resisting the temptation to exclude anyone or to privilege a certain class, era or culture, Alpers highlights the connection between the shepherd as a literary (and analytical) device and as an option for everyone to take a critical stance on their own present lives. Again, the dialogue between Meliboeus and Tityrus is presented as a key text. In Hiltner's interpretation of it, we recognise the imperative of *action* which arises as a result of the tension between sight and insight (Hiltner, 2011:37):

> Indeed, a central feature of this new version of pastoral is revealed through Meliboeus' persistent attempts to enable Tityrus both to see what he sees (to catch sight of the countryside as it falls away from him) and to feel the horror of knowing that there is little he can do to stop it.

In Alpers' version, on the other hand, Meliboeus' frustration is rather interpreted as an occasion for critical judgement. The dialogue between Meliboeus and Tityrus is carried out between two shepherds with common experience but different prospects. While Tityrus' future is safeguarded by the protection of an influential nobleman, Meliboeus is expelled from his land and just enjoys a brief stay with his old friend. As Winsor Leach notes, the privileges of Tityrus are to a large extent counterbalanced by the anxiousness of the frustrated shepherd. Nevertheless, it is exactly these challenges that give any one person, in this case Meliboeus, a chance to evaluate his or her accumulated images and develop a subjective and emancipative strength relative to the world in a final reconciliation with it.

Materialisation: keeping vital the restorative potential of a motif

The dialectics and tensions between the positive and negative ideals that are essential in pastoral *discrepancy* are likewise a premise for pastoral *emancipation*. When mobilised as a response to the present sight of a piece of land, the pastoral idealities behave like distant ancestors returning to evaluate a contemporary scene. In Alpers' view, "Vergil's exchange produces two versions of pastoral – Meliboeus', idyllic because colored by his sense of separation, and Tityrus', pragmatic and concretely rural, however protected" (Alpers, 1996:25). But in our view, this understanding of them as two versions of the pastoral overlooks the metaphorical design of the pastoral in which both sides are needed. Meliboeus articulates an ideal when he observes both the capabilities *and* the present state of the land in front of his eyes. In the negotiation between sight and insight, the potentials and realities of the current land are addressed. Any hyperbolic idealisation is modified by the instantaneous persuasion provided by the tangible land before one's eyes. Any perceived scene is framed by the aspirations and possible ideals.

The emergence into appearance of the motif in the orchard does not allow Meliboeus to escape into the memories of his former landscape, the sentimental kind of pastoral which is "difficult to define or even to locate because it is an expression less of thought than of feeling" (Marx, 2000:5). Neither does it open up any utopian scenario of the land. However, as an outcome of Meliboeus' "strength relative to the world", it is possible for him to create an insight into both the land he left and the landscape which is created in the dialogue with Tityrus. The sight of the current land sheds light on his previous condition, and the mobilisation of memories infuses the land before his eyes with meaning. The *emancipative* powers of the pastoral motif rest in a temporary escape from a potentially devastating world. As Winsor Leach remarks, "[w]hile pastoral freedom cannot exist in isolation from the great world, still the great world threatens the well-being of the country" (Leach, 1974:72). If a pastoral motif is cut off from its contemporary backdrop, the constituting tension is broken, and the motif itself becomes a dead symbol. The pastoral landscape loses its metaphorical power and ends up as a kind of degenerated *locus amoenus*, drained of its potential for meaning.

Realisation: the revealing act of seeing (distance and immediacy)

Pastoral motivation could be regarded as a longing for a comfortable lingering within previous known images. But when memory is confronted with a present and evolving nature in Meliboeus' visit to Tityrus' pastures, Meliboeus' analytical skills are used to evaluate the transitions between ever-shifting natural scenes and their antithetical backdrop. The resemblances and differences between remembered and emerging images, their arrangement according to categories such as occasion, place and context of action, are all ways of stabilising the image. We see the images with a certain attitude, but we similarly utter them with reference to a certain kind of critical reflection. Saunders notices how tightly the revealing act of seeing is bound to the synthesising act of imagining: "Indeed, it is striking how extensively both Tityrus and Meliboeus figure a number of the concrete and the more abstract features of their respective situations through the language of visual perception" (Saunders, 2008:114). The language of visual perception always works at a distance from the object that is being analysed. It is exactly the combination of the scanning eye with verbal comprehension and conceptualisation that makes visual perception such an excellent approach to landscape analysis. The analyst – Meliboeus, for instance – cannot grasp the meaning of the orchard image itself. The image is just a guiding impulse and reference, but nevertheless its presence and constitution make it possible for Meliboeus to place himself within a natural and cultural order. In a few words, Vergil lets Meliboeus narrate all his and his ancestors' engagement with land. By gesturing and naming berries, trees and fountains, he simultaneously includes these elements and the concurrent piece of land in his narrative. The dialogue between Meliboeus and Tityrus takes place *in* a landscape, but it simultaneously lets a landscape of experiences and expectations emerge into appearance to a reader. In both cases, the immediacy of the sight is framed by the distance between the opposing horizons of the two protagonists. Just as the distant hills and chimney smoke signal nightfall to the two shepherds, the prosperity of the city of Rome and Meliboeus' previous homeland represent the respective distant ideals of their talk. Regardless of how distant the experiences and prospects of the two may appear, the dialogue still continuously allows new images to appear.

When Meliboeus tries in vain to share his motif of the land with the indulgent Tityrus, the refugee is not fleeing into an image of his former life, but frames his imaging act through the sight of the land which they can both share as present. Meliboeus shows his strength by extracting ideals from his abandoned life and applying them on the present scene. The ideals derive from his subjectively experienced engagement, but additionally, he has the strength to transpose them into a new situation and let them accompany his present sensations. The image is tied to a disrupted state of being, which works as a vehicle for materialising the landscape as metaphor. The image of the land comes to visualise a lost experience as the elements lend themselves to this vision. And in the shapes of named things, they take part in the narrative which Meliboeus presents in the dialogue. Both the earlier experience and the immediate sensations must be disrupted in order to allow language to take initiative and precedence in the creation of a forward-looking landscape. His separation from habitual practice and immediate sensation provides him with a space where he is released from the constraints of repetitiousness, the routines of apprehension. There is a gap left open to be filled with an articulation of the perceived land, this time as a narrative. Meliboeus' direct confrontation of and negotiation between earlier experiences and present sensations enables him to perceive the land as a deliberate motif and to create images of present *circumstances*.

For Meliboeus, the present visibility of the motif is an instance of confirmation. The sight of the land becomes the material version of his narrative and ideals. Still, the motif is composed by nothing but the reflections of light and shade, smells and tastes, incorporated into the rhythm of his movements on the ground. The intensity of the sensations makes out a restorative *locus amoenus* within the tight net of social expectations and cultural customs. Additionally, the land becomes a scene for correction and modification. The ever-shifting material horizon represents a reliable reference for human ideas and ways of thinking. And last but not least, the intermission in the sensory realm represents a temporary suspension of thought and meaning. It lets the claims and expectations of the social and cultural world disappear for a while and strips the individual of everything but his organic presence. He lends his (invisible) finitude to the (visible) infinity of nature.

For Meliboeus, the sight reveals a material confirmation of his status in an evolving world. In his perception, however annoying, he is still capable of visualising a temporary Arcadia both despite and because of his miserable prospects. The organic unit between an individual and the ground under his or her feet lets a desirable motif emerge into appearance. As Meliboeus' statement convincingly demonstrates, only the sensing of the present land has the power to release the thought of the perfections of his ideal and to make him embrace the memories of a former life.

What we have now elaborated as a pastoral attitude has been prevalent throughout much of Western history. If we stay with Vergil, or at least some of the contemporary interpretations of his *Eclogues*, this is not an attitude which exclusively concerns the rich, powerful and privileged; it concerns anyone who openly and honestly admits the limits of his or her field of action and then is willing to uncover its present potential. The revealing act of seeing leads Meliboeus to both joyful sights and desperate insights. Alpers notes that Meliboeus' sense of loss is being displayed in his idealisation of the land. Distance and separation are the working forces at the core of this experience: "Accepting, confronting, and seeking to restore loss are normal situations for Virgil's shepherds" (Alpers, 1996:172). Winsor Leach expresses a similar opinion: "From beginning to end the poems are characterized by disappointment, frustration and lost illusion" (Leach, 1974:48). According to both Alpers' and Winsor Leach's interpretation of Vergil, the pastoral condition is one of living with loss and separation. It might be an experienced separation from a way of living or from a certain place, as in Meliboeus' case, but it might also be an imagined separation, which at its most extreme may lead someone to change his or her way of seeing the world. However that may be, the emancipatory potential of the pastoral attitude does not reside in a struggle for victory or in surrender. On the contrary, the pastoral attitude and way of acting follow the perceivable contours of a present material horizon and of knowledge obtained from individual engagement. In accordance with Rilke's words "who speaks of victory? To endure is all", pastoral emancipation is not bound to a fixed configuration, but is rather a spin-off of everyday triviality: "As a world created in imagination for the gratification of human longings, the pastoral demands a relationship with reality, either the reader's world of reality or some image contained within the poem itself" (Leach, 1974:47). The sojourn in the pastoral world, the presence of a positive ideal, does not represent a final station, but is rather a temporary suspension of the constraints of habitual life. In the pastoral tradition, however, the gap between the presence of a pastoral ideal and the experiences of ordinary life is what keeps the tension between positive and negative ideals alive. The revealing act of seeing, supported by both sensation and comprehension, may have a restorative effect.

References

Alpers, P. 1996. *What is pastoral?* Chicago, University of Chicago Press.

Cassirer, E. 1944. *An essay on man: an introduction to a philosophy of human culture,* New Haven, Yale University Press.

Hiltner, K. 2011. *What else is pastoral? Renaissance literature and the environment,* Ithaca, Cornell University Press.

Leach, E. W. 1974. *Vergil's* Eclogues: *landscapes of experience,* Ithaca, Cornell University Press.

Marx, L. 1992. Does pastoralism have a future? *In:* Hunt, J. D. (ed.) *The pastoral landscape,* Washington, DC, National Gallery of Art.

Marx, L. 2000. *The machine in the garden: technology and the pastoral ideal in America,* Oxford, Oxford University Press.

Panofsky, E. 1982. *Meaning in the visual arts,* Chicago, University of Chicago Press.

Saunders, T. 2008. *Bucolic ecology: Virgil's* Eclogues *and the environmental literary tradition,* London, Duckworth.

Chapter 3

From classical pastorals to pastoral landscapes

Rebirth of the landscape as fragile nature

Et in Arcadia ego 1999

Pastoral motivation and its three characteristic motives, which we explored in the previous chapter, are not limited to the world of ancient poetry or baroque painting. Although in many cases they operate in disguise, pastoral motives are still evident and relevant, even in contemporary landscape planning, as we shall demonstrate in what follows.

The following passage, written by Geelmuyden in 1999 (Geelmuyden, 1999), illustrates how our present idea of landscape is conditioned by inherited pastoral motifs. They are reactivated along with modernity's igrowing control over nature. The recounted event took place several years ago, during fieldwork for a project where several researchers were studying farmers' relationship to their environment, both natural and cultural. Farmers (landowners and their families) were interviewed, but the recounted episode was part of the analysis of the interviewees' farm landscapes according to a standard landscape architectural method. These expert analyses were then to be compared with the results of the interviews. The event resulted in a crisis on the part of the analyst: an exchange between the analyst's sight and the opportunity for insight about the area as landscape was obstructed by the conventions of the analytical method. The scope of the landscape analysis precluded any real *action* on the part of the analyst. This provoked a self-critical reflection and eventually a changed view of the practice of analysing landscapes. In its most successful versions, a landscape analysis does not merely present a landscape from a familiar point of view, but ends up substantially moving that very point of view. This is the case when it introduces a new horizon of comprehension whereby well-known imageries are reinterpreted and can acquire new meaning.

The introspection that was set in motion through the act of narration illustrates a pastoral attitude. For readers of the narrative today, almost 20 years later, the account's traditional motifs could be reactivated according to the three mentioned pastoral motives when interpreted in the context of their presentation at the time, as well as of their re-presentation in the context of this book.

The man with the gun: a pastoral narrative

Two years ago, on a Saturday afternoon in late September, B and I were in a small village in the upper parts of the county of Telemark in Norway, finishing a day's work of landscape inventory. It was one of those crisp autumn days, with cold and still air, a clear blue sky, and an autumn sun that baked the cut meadows and set birch and aspen aflame in a blaze of yellows and reds. We had driven up there to map and take pictures of ten farms. Earlier that same summer, a colleague of ours had visited those ten farms and interviewed the farmers there. She had talked to each of them, and sometimes also to their spouses, for several hours, about their relationship with and feelings for the cultural remains and landscape in their community and around their own farms. B and I had been quite surprised when we had realised that morning that she had not said anything to her interviewees about our coming later on in the autumn. Whether it was that realisation or some other observation that made me feel uneasy, I still cannot tell. It was a feeling of not being welcome, of not having any legitimate reason to be there. That uneasiness did not pass for the whole day. We met several people: they were out in the fine weather, working on or around their houses. Most greeted us with a kind of aloof curiosity: who were we and what was our business?

The sun had gone across the sky and stood low, casting its last rays but barely heating the hillside on which most of the farms we had seen were perched. We were climbing up a steep and winding dirt road in B's car, passing steep meadows and gradually thinning spruce forest. Finally, after a sharp left turn, the road flattened out and stopped. To the left of us, some ten metres down the slope, facing the valley and the evening sun, lay the farmstead in question, our object of investigation. What a beautiful sight/ site! There were five buildings clustered on the upper edge of a meadow which, as it seemed to me, had not been cut for many years. Yellow, thin straws of dry grass were moving in the slight breeze, catching the day's last sunlight. The buildings, all wooden, and with wood shingle or corrugated iron roofs, had not been painted or otherwise tended to for a long time. They were glowing in a warm grey-brown in this light. But there was no sense of abandonment or dilapidation; I'd rather say that there was a sense of loneliness, and even timelessness: the circle of the seasons seemed to be the only relevant time denominator. Somebody lived there: there were red geraniums and white lace curtains in the windows of the dwelling. A narrow path had been mowed from the post where a mailbox hung where we had parked our car, and when we got down into the farmyard we saw that the entrance door was slightly open.

B went down and knocked on the door while I stood waiting in the middle of the yard, camera in hand, but only taking in the atmosphere of the place. I heard B call "hello" once, saw her push the door a little more open saying "hello" again. No answer. She came back, saying she had heard someone in there, and that the person had withdrawn into the house.

"They don't want us here," I said. "We should get out of the yard". B took a picture. I was a little faster in my retreat back up to the car.

We both thought that we couldn't leave without at least a few pictures and notes, if only from a little distance. So we walked along a path on the upper edge of the farmstead so that we could get a look at it as a whole from the side, without intruding. The unusual beauty and peacefulness of the place contrasted dramatically with the feeling inside me. I was scared.

"Let's get out of here," I said and started walking back to the car. B followed me, but when we reached the mailbox, where a tailless cat now sat watching us, she decided she needed a few more pictures from the other side of the farm. I did not like the idea of staying there, but on the other hand I was aware that the fear I felt was entirely my own, that there had not been any actual incident to warrant it. B was obviously not feeling the same thing. I thought I must be going mad, that I was getting tired and that the uneasiness I had been feeling all day was playing tricks on me. As I opened the passenger door, I inadvertently looked down into the farmyard. I suddenly caught sight of the upper part of the body of a man walking across the yard, carrying what looked like a potted plant by its branches in his right hand. We saw each other simultaneously, held each other's eyes for what couldn't have been more than a tenth of a second; without a nod or any other kind of acknowledgement he disappeared behind a tree, and I sat in the car. I sat waiting, noting down the configuration of the buildings in relation to each other and to the surrounding meadows and the observation that the forest above the farm had been grazed not more than maybe ten or 15 years ago. I also sat wondering at how different this place seemed from the one we had visited just before, although many physical characteristics – such as the type and number of buildings, the situation on the valley slope etc. – were essentially the same. I also remember thinking that B should hurry up.

Then I was suddenly startled by a sharp and loud sound. I looked up and around me, but couldn't see anything. I remember associating the sound with the flowerpot I had seen the man carry, and I had a notion that what I had heard was the pot being flung violently into a metal barrel. But I must have been puzzled by the strangeness or unlikeliness of that notion: I could not settle on it as the right "picture" for the sound I had heard.

"Or was it a shot?" I can remember myself wondering next, and as I sat contemplating that possibility (I haven't heard many shots in my life, so I really wasn't sure), I heard a man's angry shouting from down by the farmhouse. I couldn't see anything there, but when I looked back behind the car, I saw B walking resolutely towards me, looking down, apparently ignoring the person who was shouting at her (us) not far from her to the left.

"He shot at me," was the first thing she said when she had sat down behind the steering wheel. It seemed to take her an eternity to get the car started, turned around and heading away. It was only with great effort that I was able to hide the impatience I felt: it seemed like she was moving in slow motion, but I didn't say a word!

It wasn't until we had gone a way back down the road that B said: "He was standing at the corner of the house pointing his rifle at me all the way while I was walking back to the car."

Back home again, on the following Monday, B called the local police and told them about the incident. That surprised me: I realised that I hadn't thought of doing that myself. I somehow felt that the man had had a right to shoot.

Landscape as cultural idea: image of unity between humanity and nature

First of all, this account clearly shows a place perceived as *landscape*. The narrator (A) engages with the land in a certain way, relating to it according to a landscape idea as well as a landscape ideal. She presents an image framed as beautiful and peaceful, where the emphasis is on the natural and rural features of the site, a farmyard high on a mountain slope in Norway during a sunny and warm autumn afternoon; there are signs of abandoned grazing and neglected mowing, indicating a gradual renaturation of the place. Human culture is present in the form of a tidy yard, old farmhouses, lace curtains etc. Additionally, ephemeral elements lend more life and a certain drama to the scene: low afternoon sunlight, autumn colours, moving grass, a tailless cat. Even tactile qualities, smells (baked) and sounds are mentioned to a certain degree.

The analysts arrive at the farmstead with a cultural and visual baggage, which, importantly, they take for granted: in a quasi-instinctive fashion, they see the farmstead with a gaze formed through the pictorial template of traditional landscape motifs in art, as they can be observed in any gallery with Norwegian landscape paintings such as *Seljefløiten*. What we are dealing with is a *landscape narrative* modelled on the pastoral tradition, visual and literary.

Classical pastoral models

One of the *earliest known* pictorial renderings of pastoral beauty in sensuous terms is Martini Simone's (1284–1344) frontispiece for his close friend Petrarch's favourite copy of Vergil's *Eclogues and Georgics*. It is, the art historian Kenneth Clark contends, "the first time since antiquity [that] the pursuits of country life are represented as a source of happiness and poetry" (Clark, 1961:6).

According to Clark, the actual *model* for all later pastoral landscapes in visual art was first defined in the paintings of Giorgione (1477–1510) and Titian (1488–1576), complete with shepherds, nymphs and satyrs lounging on flowery meadows with animals, musical instruments and easily accessible fruit meals, and set within a frame of rockery and overarching trees. These scenes are also held together, occasionally, by the enrapturing dreamlike gaze of one of the figures, but always by the unifying principle of light, such as the drama of a thundery sky or a golden sunset. The imagery was adopted and developed in the 17th century's rediscovery of Arcadia, by Nicolas Poussin (1594–1665), Claude Lorrain (1600–1682) and others. The influence of the two mentioned painters' compositions on the first English landscape gardens and the subsequent appreciation of landscapes as beautiful, picturesque and sublime, as well as on the aesthetics of landscapes today, is undisputed (Clark, 1961; Hunt, 1992; Andrews, 1999; Ruff, 2015). As Clark states (Clark, 1961:70):

> There was something in Claude's gentle poetry, in his wistful glances at a vanished civilization and in his feeling that all nature could be laid out for man's delight, like a gentleman's park, which appealed particularly to the English connoisseurs of the eighteenth century.

Clark's statement on Claude Lorrain points to several aspects of these pastoral paintings as the possible cause of their great impact, and we shall elaborate on these below.

The birth of landscape in modernity

It is in Renaissance painting that what was originally a setting, a background landscape, gradually emerged as the main subject (Andrews, 1999:25–53). Originally, what was termed "landscapes" *were* paintings (Trepl, 2012:40). Clark describes the development of landscape into an artistic genre in its own right as marked by two characteristics. One is the transition from a "state of mind, in which all material objects were thought of as symbols of spiritual truths or episodes in sacred history" (Clark, 1961:3) into an attention to God's creation as a display of beautiful patterns. The other is that Nature thus could be conceptualised as decorative and for the first time emerged into appearance as "landscape".

The transformation of vision that occurred in the Renaissance did not take place on a tabula rasa. In the 14th and 15th centuries, Petrarch and others had rediscovered and started emulating Greek and Roman classics such as the poetry of Ovid (43 BCE – 17 CE) and Vergil (70–19 BCE), first in Latin, then in Italian, as in Boccaccio's *Decamerone* (1353) and Sannazarro's *Arcadia* (1480–1504). Petrarch owned several copies of one of the first pieces of literature of the kind to be (later) termed pastoral, Vergil's *Eclogues* (ca. 40 BCE), which together with another of the poet's major works, the *Georgics* (ca. 30 BCE) has had a lasting influence on Western art and the culture of landscape (Ruff, 2015; Hunt and Willis, 1988; Hunt, 1992).

In a famous analysis, the German philosopher Joachim Ritter (Ritter, 1974) designates Petrarch's reflection in a letter to his brother on his ascent of Mont Ventoux in April 1336 as the very first instance of a landscape experience in our modern sense. Ritter characterises the novelty of Petrarch's description of the view as follows: "Nature therefore becomes landscape only when a human 'goes out' into nature in order to take part 'out there' in her in free delighting observation and thus take part in the 'Whole' which presents itself in and as Nature" (Ritter, 174:147, our translation).

Whole *Nature* becomes aesthetic *nature in paintings and gardens*

According to Ritter (Ritter, 1974), the aesthetic appreciation of nature as landscape grew out of the *theoria* tradition in Greek philosophy, which is a reflection on "Cosmos", the world of the gods and of humans' partaking in that imagined *Whole* of *Nature*. It subsumes but transcends the practical world of need fulfilment, as it still depends on philosophy or, as it were, religion, rather than on what is "out there" in the physical world for its articulation as holistic entity; but from the 13th century on, humanity's concept of nature acquires a new, more sensuous shape. In Ritter's words, modernity developed a special "organ" whereby the concept of whole nature (Cosmos) was relocated: no longer in philosophical/religious thought, as it had been before along with everything else, but in *aesthetic experience*, in Our translation the landscapes of poetry and art, freed of all sense of utility, alongside and apart from the emerging sciences' concept of nature (Ritter, 1974:34):

> In contrast to the natural sciences' world of non-metaphorical objects, aesthetic nature, landscape, has taken over the role of conveying the whole of nature and the harmony of the Cosmos, in the shape of intuitable images, such as arise out of inner human worlds [paraphrasing Alexander von Humboldt's (1844) theory of Cosmos].

Similarly, the garden historian John Dixon Hunt finds proof of the awakened sense of the garden as a "third nature" in two letters from the 16th century describing villas in northern Italy (Hunt, 2000). This is a nature where aesthetics plays the main role, set off from the surrounding landscape of agriculture and wilderness. Both agricultural and wild landscapes, now in a stylised form, were incorporated in the symbolic arrangements of the garden. Gardens thereby became a new pastoral form of expression: their scenes were modelled on the pastoral scenes of Vergil, as they were being interpreted in both writings and the newly available array of painted pastoral images following his poems' coming into print in the late 15th century. Conversely, however, Clark also holds that garden art itself from very early on had been conducive to the symbolic representations of nature and countryside in painting. It had provided a "compass of the imagination, and itself a symbol of perfection. [...] Its reappearance in the twelfth century is only a part of the reawakening of the imaginative faculty" (Clark, 1961:4).

Pastoral *landscapes*, understood as painterly motifs *and* garden scenes, now become the prototypical ideal of the pastoral idea of an undivided and harmonious humanity-nature relationship. As recorded by Hunt (Hunt and Willis, 1988) in the context of the development of the English landscape garden, the painterly models of Lorrain and Poussin offered critics such as Joseph Addison, Stephen Switzer, Alexander Pope and several others a visual language with which to articulate the experience of the Italian villa gardens that they had travelled to and admired. This was a new kind of cultural engagement in nature, which the simultaneously emerging natural sciences on the one hand, and a technical-economic attitude to the environment on the other, could not represent and had to leave behind. This is also, of course, what is still reflected in landscape as a vernacular term today (Benediktsson, 2007), where it basically means a (mostly pleasant) view of a tract of land.

Pastoral motives invested in modern pastoral landscapes

As with Petrarch, what A and B see in the view as they drive up the hill to the farmstead is not a farmer's nature, nor that of an engineer. Nor, however, is it a nature that God has given them and to which they feel unconditionally and forever subjected. It is a nature that they, and we as readers, can appreciate with the senses of citizens of a welfare state enjoying the benefits of modern technology and economy as well as an urban lifestyle. They are symbolic shepherds that are here enjoying and pointing to the setting sun, the meadows, etc. It is a nature which one reaches out into for a certain kind of rest and personal re-creation.

However, the account also conveys its landscape image through a strong narrative plot: two people visit the farm, intending to conduct an analysis of it as landscape for research purposes; they have driven a car to the end of a steep winding road and a magnificent view is revealed; they have notebooks and cameras. The inhabitant of the farm declines their invitation to talk and later shows overt hostility, firing a gun and shouting at them. The gratifying aesthetic idyll turns into drama.

In philosopher Martin Seel's words, the idea of landscape has developed as a medium through which society can negotiate its relationship with a "problematic nature" (Seel, 1996:25), a nature that we are free to act in relation to and thereby must problematise. A problematic relationship to nature, according to Seel and others (Ritter, 1974; Groh and Groh, 1991), is a precondition for "nature seen as landscape". This does not imply that people did not enjoy the beauties of nature before the Renaissance; Seel's thesis is that it did not become a *cultural idea* before that time in history.

Negotiating a problematic nature

As we saw in chapter two, the idealizing aspect of the pastoral legacy is only one of its traits: it also carries with it a reflective and critical subtext. The Renaissance's rediscovery of the ancient works happened at a historical moment when humans were again becoming aware of their possibilities as free and observant agents in relation to an external nature. Their poems' natural scenes with fruit trees and fields are drawn attention to by shepherds as symbols of a happier and more secure life, seen in contrast to the city's political scheming, a lost homeland or a forsaken love.

Being himself exiled from Rome and at odds with the politics of the Church, Petrarch had recognised the politically critical aspect of Vergil's *Eclogues*. Similarly, the English rediscovery of Renaissance literature's adoption of antiquity's pastorals again happened at a time when new visions were called for. The old narratives' underlying motives regained acute relevance in 16th-century England, as old ways of life and the landscapes they had created were for ever disappearing, along with an expanding world of explored natures and regions, and the increasing speed and scale of their exploitation. It was in fact only with this 16th-century recognition of Renaissance interpretations that the pastoral was conceptualised *as tradition* (Andrews, 1999:65). It is through its intrinsic critical motivation that the pastoral tradition has been able to flower and gain new momentum again and again, especially in times of economic and political change or unrest.

Despite the general recognition of the above-mentioned *visual model*'s great influence on the development of the English landscape vision, Hunt (Hunt and Willis, 1988) draws attention to the fact that the pastoral painters themselves relied upon a rich *narrative* pastoral tradition. Its literary motifs were simultaneously being adapted to contemporary Christian pastoral life by poets and followers of Petrarch and other Renaissance pastoralists. Hunt contends that no less influential than paintings for the development of the English garden were pastoral works such as Spenser's *The Shepheardes Calender* (1579), *Paradise Lost* by John Milton (1667), and country house poems such as Ben Jonson's *To Penshurst* (1616) or Andrew Marvell's *Upon Appleton House* (1681). Clark confirms this when he postulates of Poussin and Lorrain that they do not "at all suggest the imaginative world of Ovid and Virgil. They are too grave, too weighted down with thought and the consciousness of the original sin" (Clark, 1961:68).

Along with its reinterpretation in the central and northern European culture of the 17th century, the mythological Arcadia was merging with the idea of the Garden of Eden as it was *now* imagined against the dramatic physical changes and cultural reorientations that were taking place, especially in the English and the Dutch empires, albeit in different ways in the two countries (Ruff, 2015). Whereas the English garden owners' realisations of ideal pastoral landscapes were part of their identification with Roman dignitaries and the great ancient empire, the rising class of Dutch mercantile rulers aspired to the grandeur of other European countries' aristocracies. The painted landscapes they commissioned were less idealising: "not entirely imaginary, often they were set in a specifically local setting, or at least an imagined reality" (Ruff, 2015:56). The Dutch republic realised its Arcadia through the celebration of its own prosperous rural regions as they were developing in parallel with and at the periphery of its growing and prolific towns. In both the English and Dutch cases, one can detect a certain nostalgia for a changing rural countryside, but it carried different symbolism in the two nations' self-understandings. The ideal English garden landscapes were also a statement against the absolutisms of the French monarchy and the papal Church. The landscapes of Dutch Calvinists, on the other hand, showed everyday landscapes with all their realistic details, revealing a country in the making and concerned with the special character of its own countryside. As Allan Ruff observes, these landscapes "were not populated with nymphs, satyrs and the other deities of nature like Pan, for the simple reason that the beauties of the Dutch landscape were considered sufficient" (Ruff, 2015:64).

Negotiating a problematic self: an evolving culture of vision

As we have argued, seeing landscapes has never been a purely physiological reaction but a shaping and constructing act, an attempt to inhabit the land through the eyes. As cultural phenomenon, landscape perception thus develops in parallel with increased power, independence and secularisation, a growing cultural and psychological capital; but on the other hand, becoming conscious of this acquired power and freedom also suggests a responsibility: with no more divine force to blame for unwanted change, disasters and misfortunes, the need for absolution from the burden of having to exert proper (environmental) agency gradually becomes an essential aspect of cultural modernity, on a cultural as well as individual level (Marquard, 1981).

In the wake of the Industrial Revolution's dramatic changes to social life as well as the environment, the pastoral tradition offered a vital body of narratives and images that allowed the tension between the affirmation of an existing national and individual self and a renewal of that very self to take on new forms.

The invention of the central perspective in Renaissance Italy had marked an important step in the culture of landscape (Clark, 1961; Panofsky, 1991; Wellmer, 1985; Roger, 1997), establishing a mathematical relationship between land, eye and medium. The seamless incorporation of selected elements of nature into their physical surroundings, their milieu, enabled them to be seen at an appropriate distance, as part of a larger, naturalistically rendered whole. With the invention of the microscope in 17th century Holland, the smallest details of natural processes became visible and explainable. The medium through which the humanity-nature relationship is *presented* as landscape, be it pictures or words, is constitutive of the way we see landscapes, and the awareness of land as landscape coincides with an awareness of how humans have explored, discovered and controlled vision.

The rediscovery, naming and subsequent appropriation of earlier pastoral works coincided with the humanity-nature relationship's also becoming a prime concern in modern philosophical aesthetics, as first articulated by the Earl of Shaftesbury (1737), explicated by Baumgarten (1750), and finally fully developed by Kant (1790). Baumgarten is the first to emphasise the *effect* that nature has on humans and thereby opens a space for the *individual* interpretation of nature in aesthetic terms. In that it becomes objectified as landscape in the arts, the ideal image of a humanity-nature unity can be looked upon as both a *given* convention and at the same time, in the immediate landscape experience, as something that the individual *creates* in perception. The *sublime* is a landscape idea which grew out of this modern sensibility as an extension of and reaction to the *beautiful* (Beardsley and Beardsley, 1966:182):

> The willingness to look and feel opened the eye to the delights of [nature's] more wild and fearsome aspects: rugged cliffs, chasms, raging torrents – and the appalling vastness of interstellar space. Out of the broadening of appreciation grew the deeper concept of the sublime.

Landscape *ideals* visualise a problematic gap between culture's productions (*work*) and evolving nature as the entirely Other. In modernity's landscape idea, seeing is metaphorically transformed into "re-cognition" of history's relentless changes, of time passing, of the ephemerality of humans' existence as outsiders, set against, but also as involved insiders of the eternal world of nature. Nature seen as landscape thus becomes a space for the unrepresentable, in nature and in the self, an internalised place for the activities of contemplation and search in themselves. Such is the boy's experience in the woods in the poem *Tonen,* and such is the experience evidenced in all the iconic works of the pastoral tradition (Clark, 1961:65):

> The Virgilian element in Claude is, above all, his sense of a Golden age, of grazing flocks, unruffled waters and a calm luminous sky, images of perfect harmony between man and nature, but touched, as he combines them, with a Mozartian wistfulness, as he knew that perfection could last no longer than the moment in which it takes possession of our minds.

Even as perceptions, landscapes are artworks "in stadu nascendi", that is, in the process of being born, the landscape ecologist Ludwig Trepl declares

(Trepl, 2012:40). Any objective landscape presentation, be it in words, a picture or otherwise, already contains the germ of its own dissolution and the beginning of a reframing of the world. The landscape idea must be understood as a *culture of seeing human liminality*. The constant necessity to redefine the positive ideal of humanity-nature unity in relation to a *contemporary* and actual human alienation from nature is immanent to pastoral landscapes.

Negotiating human liminality

In the gunshot account, we might read the mentioned unease juxtaposed with the exquisite beauty and peace of the day as indicating a snake in the shadows, like that in Vergil's third *Eclogue*. The snake here is the recognition of the lack of a common horizon of comprehension. What is displayed is a confrontation between different landscapes, just like that between Tityrus and Meliboeus in Vergil's first *Eclogue*: the symbolic image of the area held by the researchers on the one hand, and that held by the inhabitant on the other. We can also attach the perceived beauty of the farmstead in Telemark to the noted motifs of abandoned grazing and neglected mowing, which indicate a beginning renaturation of the place. These are reminiscent of the more general motif of the *ruin*, "an active ingredient of threat or tension in [the] visual pastoral" (Hunt, 1992:15), which gained emblematic meaning especially in garden art, as a visualisation of human life's (and culture's) eventual death confronted with the eternity of nature's processes. According to Hunt, "tensions between imagery of peace, ease, and rural refuge and some internal [...] or external [...] threat to them, [...] lies between the confident assertion of stability and the socio-economic climate in which it is *uttered*" (Hunt, 1992:15, our emphasis). Seen from the periphery – that is, the rural countryside and the man in the account – death *is* imminent: life as it was until the 1960s has disappeared and changed into something altogether new, where the quality of the place is being reduced to its picturesque attractiveness to weekend tourists and cottage owners, or as cultural heritage artefacts to landscape architects and historians, here represented by the two researchers. But there are also hints at differences between the two researchers, between A's and B's attitudes, the latter showing fewer scruples regarding their professional mission. In other words, we can also catch sight of a dialectic between the self-evidence with which the researchers are initially prepared to apply their method of analysis and a beginning, less confident self-awareness. Unlike B, the narrator seems to vaguely realise as problematic that her vision is guided by a learnt but currently inappropriate ideal where rural landscape beauty is connected to small dairy farm landscapes, natural botanical succession to waning biological diversity, and abandoned farming to cultural heritage artefacts.

In the design of the research project as a whole, new knowledge was expected to emerge from the comparison of results from farmer interviews with the experts' conventional landscape analyses and evaluations. Thus, the narrator's emerging awareness was not something that came out of the experience alone: a critical attitude to expert methods of landscape analysis was integral to the project's investigative perspective and research design. A new idea of landscape was interfering with A's image of the site, that is, disturbing her habitual way of imaging a landscape.

To a certain degree, the project was part of the so-called cultural or linguistic turn in landscape studies that began in the 1980s, as mentioned in chapter one. An inherent tension had emerged as a demarcating quality of landscape as expression of the modern human engagement with land (Wylie, 2007). It was framed as various dichotomies or dialectics, such as those between insiders and outsiders (Relph, 1976), between sight or experience and representation (Hirsch and O'Hanlon, 1996; Corner, 1991), subjective place and objective space (Relph, 1976; Tuan, 1977), picture and process (Andrews, 1999), actuality and potentiality (Hirsch and O'Hanlon, 1996; Corner, 1990) and others. We can identify them as different aspects of modernity's landscape liminality: discrepancies that manifest an actualised pastoral confrontation between a positive and a negative ideal and motivate the emergence into appearance of a landscape.

In the landscape images and narratives of modernity, landscape thus visualises a state of constantly re-actualised pastoral liminality. Looking at art, the art historian Malcom Andrews for instance contends that from one point of view, "[l]andscape art in the West, over the last 500 years, can be read as the elegiac record of humanity's sense of alienation from its original habitat in an irrecoverable, pre-capitalist world" (Andrews, 1999:21). From today's point of view, however, he continues: "We don't have to imagine, with the aid of alluring images of Arcadian natural simplicity, what it must have been like to live *in* Nature; we are all too aware of our dependency on nature now" (Andrews, 1999:22). The last decades' landscape art, therefore, discards the idea of "landscape as a way of seeing from a distance" in favour of an idea of landscape as our *environment* and as *processes*, both of which, importantly, implicate human agency. Andrews connects the aesthetic dimension of the landscape idea to the realm of ethics. Pastoral landscape representations perform a gesture: they utter a critical point of view towards some aspect of a situation by holding it up against a more desired situation. Andrews emphasises landscape art's *narrative arguments*: what they are is dramatically expressed in the conclusion of his book (Andrews, 1999:223):

> For the last 500 years western landscape art has been like a barometer of anxieties over the balance between nature and culture. We have come to realize that nature – that "out there", that "other" – is not necessarily perpetually self-renewing. It is more like ourselves than we ever feared. When it is not offering us green spaces as utopian as ever the

most artificial pastoral managed to be, landscape art in our times comes burdened with guilt.

As the shot and shouting on the afternoon in Telemark interrupt the harmony in the scene, the initially felt lack of welcome turns into fear and a finale in the form of escape. In the hindsight of the account, the narrator is puzzled by her own reactions to the experience: she does not blame the shooter. By activating the pastoral motive of discrepancy, we can now conceptualise the Telemark episode as liminal, and the final astonished realisation and suspended judgement as an emergence into appearance of the *described* conventional image of the place as a beginning *new insight*.

As we look back at the Telemark account's pastoral plot and our interpretation of its image as symbolic ruin from *the two researchers'* perspective, it is not death itself that lurks in it as the negative ideal. In narrating the experience, A embarks on an analysis of this landscape and becomes conscious of herself, in the role of a conventional analyst, as part of the picture, as a person creating a certain version of reality through the act of analysing.

From sight to insight: methodological liminality

As the confrontation between A's and B's attitudes in Telemark emerges as the most relevant discrepancy within the image at the time of its utterance, the scope of analysis is moved away from the *area* to an image that is contingent on the tool for its representation, in this case the analytical method itself. The symbolic ruin here, then, is not the buildings and meadows themselves, but rather their *status as chosen motif*. This became an opportunity to catch sight of a new horizon of comprehension, which was that the idea of landscape itself is intrinsic to *the way* a landscape is represented, for instance in an analysis.

Landscape as symbolic ruin

The narrator's enraptured gaze can be associated with the shepherds' reaction in Nicolas Poussin's second (Louvre) version of *Et in Arcadia ego* (Figure 2.3): just as Poussin's shepherds confront a discrepancy between the depicted peaceful scene and a negative aspect of the situation, a negative ideal is opposed to a positive one, a reflection (*action*) takes place and moves the image onto a new, conceptual level. This same switch from depicted agents' condition of *labour* via *work* to *action* is traced by Panofsky in his analysis of the transition from the first (Figure 2.2) to the second version of Poussin's *Et in Arcadia ego*: the second (Louvre) version "no longer shows a dramatic encounter with Death but a contemplative absorption in the idea of mortality" (Panofsky, 1982:313). This painting is meant to act differently from the first version, where the figures are taken literally, as Hiltner

(Hiltner, 2011) would have said. Whereas in the first (Chatsworth) version we are, as spectators, invited into the scene and encouraged to perform the imaginative act of the shepherds with them, in the second (Louvre) version they must be interpreted as a tableau: the entire painting acts as an illustration of a finished and fulfilled *thought*, the utterance of a clear insight. *It* becomes the image and outcome of the utterance (*action*) itself, whose legitimacy, however, lies in its ability to call forth memories of common human reactions (*labour*) and known motifs (*work*). This is also what we saw demonstrated in Bjørnson's poem in our introductory chapter.

Through the utterance of an analytical narrative (*action*) of the gunshot episode, a new version of the pastoral ideal emerges. As landscape, the farmstead in Telemark can only regain meaning as *symbolic* ruin when treated as the *point of view* with which the analysts first encounter the scene: it is a point of view which can be expressed through known landscape motifs, whose meaning, however, is in a constant process of dying and being reborn. This is what the ruin, and ultimately any pastoral landscape, symbolises. It is the image of the insight that the humanity-nature relationship is in a constant state of liminality. James Corner contends that we should think of landscape architecture as "the practice of e-scaping and rescaping our relationship to nature and the 'other' through the construction of built worlds" (Corner, 1991:129).

Whereas one could say that modern landscape *art* and to some degree landscape design have evolved as continuous explorations and visualisations of that liminality in their inherent call for *subjective* contemplations and manifest utterances on the culture-nature relationship (Meyer, 1998; Czerniak, 1997; Herrington, 2006), the development has taken an altogether different turn in landscape planning. As the beautiful, sublime and picturesque were concretised in garden views, and the ideal garden gradually became increasingly nature-like in its physical appearance, it quasi-effaced itself as artifice. The contemporary discourses that followed these landscape ideas were all soon forgotten and their respective idealised images were *naturalised* as *the* ways of perceiving a site as landscape. This naturalisation of a certain point of view also cemented a certain conceptual point of view and horizon of comprehension (Ellison, 2013).

Within the frame of European history of thought, Trepl (Trepl, 2012) contends that this radical change in the cultural conception of nature was set in motion in the late 18th century, and has since influenced how we have come to look at and treat the land as landscapes in planning. In an era of new national consolidations, the political-philosophical movement of conservatism, especially the philosophy of Gottfried Herder and its reception in the 19th century, was conducive to the idea that land and people ideally constitute a harmonious and organic whole, where humankind cultivates its God-given skills in order to bring out the natural potentials in its native land. Thereby a perfect, harmonious and characteristic objective unity between every human/culture and nature would be created, resulting in the uniqueness as well as the diversity of cultural landscapes. Cosgrove provides the following diagnosis of the situation in England more than a century later (Cosgrove, 1998:xxiii):

> British debates over planning and controlling the impacts of a modern industrial state and post-war reconstruction at mid-century turned in very considerable measure on maintaining continuity in the appearance of the land, not merely for aesthetic ends but out of a sustained and widely-held belief that orderly landscape was both cause and consequence of a morally ordered civic society seeking to negotiate the changes wrought by modern living.

This philosophical stance has had far-reaching consequences, such as in the observing attitude to cultural landscapes promoted by Carl Sauer (Wylie, 2007) in geography, and not the least in the methods for legitimising decisions that were developed in landscape planning with the modernist collapse of history's models and the embrace of ecology (McHarg, 1992). In both these approaches, a value-free way of observing landscape has gained prevalence. Whereas *landscape* in the quotation above still comes across as a clearly human way of *voicing* an image of reality as symbolic, an ideal in contrast to a current obstacle to it, in the meantime it has been reduced to a pictorial (or other) *model* through the method that brings it into materialisation, in planning documents or in the arrangement of sites themselves.

Landscape as object of planning: landscape *into* land

Landscape has reverted into *land* in the context of environmental planning, but in a rather different manner than in the arts, where as we saw, the ethical dimension of landscape, its implication of human agency, is being foregrounded. On the one hand, landscape has undergone a differentiation into different natural science concepts; and on the other, landscape has become banalised as people's opinions or preferences concerning the physical appearance of the land. Neither the development in the arts nor the framing of landscape as *tension* in cultural geography and anthropology have been able to prevent this development. The reason for this might be their shortcoming that they have not been able to connect to the practice of landscape analysts and planners, or to their role as active agents with an obligation to provide landscape proposals in concrete public decision-making processes.

The need to stabilise landscape ideals' evanescence and arrive at a firm "ground zero" from where visions can be drawn up and decisions for a better future can be legitimised is what has motivated the development of methods of landscape analysis in planning since the 1960s. The question has been: on what aesthetic, *landscape* grounds can a change be proposed or a public decision made? This is the question that also lay at the bottom of the research that was being carried out in Telemark.

The preservation documents designating Dælivannet, the site of Skredsvig's painting, as worthy of protection illustrate how this question has been dealt with in planning (Miljøverndepartementet, 1978). As we saw in the introduction, the documents mix verbal and visual media and present an inventory of landscape qualities and particularly protected elements within a larger cultural landscape, thus constituting *different scientific* landscapes. On the other hand, seen as a whole, the documents convey an overall image with aesthetic attractiveness and cultural meaning, the contemporary relevance of which, however, is not explained. As in the landscape image of the Telemark account, we recognise a way of seeing and valuing areas developed within the arts, architecture and landscape architecture after the Renaissance, that is, strongly influenced by the aesthetic ideals of the picturesque, beautiful and sublime as formulated within 17th-century theory of garden and landscape art. The description method's argumentative power relies on a convention of landscape appreciation, which is, however, no longer explicit. We may associate it with concepts such as "ecosystem services" and "biological diversity", which in turn can be associated with political agendas such as, "ecological and social sustainability", "increased sense of identity" and "human well-being", concepts that Allan Ruff has dubbed *Arcadia revisited* (Ruff, 2015:231). Paradoxically, however, whereas the overall landscape planning approach's rationale seems to be that a landscape is more than the sum of elements and artefacts in an area, the arguments for protecting the Dælivannet area nevertheless emerge as a summing up of objects to be safeguarded against any activity that might result in a change of its unspecified "type or character" (Miljøverndepartementet, 1978:3).

The impossibility of a technocratic Arcadia

We are reminded of Marx's powerful metaphor of *The machine in the garden* (Marx, 2000), albeit inverted: Dælivannet is a garden in the suburban machine of Bærum with its urbanised lifestyle and its incessant and rapid territorial transformations. As his title indicates, Marx points out the *machine* as the active counterforce in pastoral imaginary idealisation. In his words, the symbolic power of a pastoral motif "brings the political and the psychic dissonance associated with the onset of industrialism into a single pattern of meanings" (Marx, 2000:30). Here, however, the original value reference – the *idea* of the Dælivannet landscape as garden, in contrast to the negative ideal of the omnipresent instruments of an urbanised, commodified and regulated world – is not only left unarticulated, but is even *subverted*: in the representation of it as an asset in the service of humankind, an "affordance", an "ecological service", or as interesting data that are computable and representable in the virtual realities of maps.

The presented holistic landscape has fallen apart into a number of conceptualisations of it as objective nature and/or physical land features on a map; the painting's interest appears to lie in the area-features that it depicts; and by creating the illusion that the site has always looked as it does in the painting, the whole scene at Dælivannet reinforces an idea of the depicted *land features* as the *landscape* of Dælivannet. As mere pictorial ideal, it has been disconnected from the original idea of landscape, where an ideal is inseparably juxtaposed with its negation in some form. Just as at the farmstead in Telemark, the ruin's symbolism of a tension or dialectics is no longer active as such when it has been reduced to the picturesqueness of the literal buildings, meadows, ditches and trees of a site. The material ruin is mistaken for the symbolic ruin. Landscape has become a static, dead motif. In Hunt's words, we have come to "see the signifier and not the signified" (Hunt, 1992:15).

Since Cosgrove's observations above, planning has developed a paradoxical attitude to landscape. We can recognise this paradox in the European Landscape Convention (Council of Europe, 2000:6c). Its stated values and goals are strangely at odds with its mandate to the ratifying countries to identify their territories' characteristic landscapes through landscape assessment (Geelmuyden and Fiskevold, 2016). In the Convention's Norwegian translation, the term "identify" is translated as "mapping", but even where this is not the case, the term has been interpreted in that way in many countries. This has led to the production of "landscape character maps" or similar territorial inventories (Brunetta and Voghera, 2008) whose validity, however, is not limited by any "best before" date.

The resulting landscapes' *character* is that they are ahistorical. They are also narrowly instrumental, in that they posit humanity as a neutral observer and rely on ever more "sophisticated" technical tools that promise easy "solutions" to the enigmatic task of understanding areas as landscapes. Within this heuristic, landscape increasingly becomes a technical term, a tool for efficient place production: the area is seen as landscape because a relatively *large scale* of investigation is applied. The various experts work on a "landscape scale", as opposed to for instance a "species scale" in ecology (Marburger and Forman, 1997), an "object scale" in archaeology (Ramenofsky and Steffen, 1998; Huggett, 2015) or a "detail scale" in geography (Selman, 2006).

With today's powerful digitised mapping, representation and tracking technologies, the task of analysing landscapes is being transformed into a question of accurate measurement and sufficient data. The science-inspired methodology's landscape concepts, imposing a solidified landscape ideal on everyone, reveals itself as no longer realisable in the contemporary context of trying to gain insight from a landscape. The methods inherently dissolve the ideal of a humanity-nature-unity (Geelmuyden, 1989:242). Their landscape concept is no longer sustainable. It has become a new version of the "machine" in the garden (Marx, 2000), the negative ideal we are faced with today. Landscape planning has reached an aporia, as foreseen by Erwin

Straus many years ago: "The more modern life succumbs to technology, the stronger the longing becomes for landscape, the more forced/desperate the effort to regain it becomes, and – strangely enough – to regain it by means of technology" (Straus, 1956:339, our translation). Just a few years before the Telemark account was written, Alain Roger (Roger, 1997) had declared that we have a "crisis of landscape", because we are witnessing a crisis in the "double artialisation of nature, in situ and in visu", that is, on site and through sight, which must be a continuing human activity. In Roger's words, we are working with "displaced/dis-landscaped" models of seeing (*dépaysés/ dépaysagés*, Roger, 1997:113), ideals that are outdated and defunct in a post-industrial globalised world and that have lost their essential connection to our imaginative powers. The underlying value base of landscape as image of an ideal humanity-nature harmony has been left unpronounced for so long now that the dynamism of landscape, as images uttered in a situated dialogue, has been lost. The boy's melody seems to have been drowned in a cacophony of loud instruments; and the question is whether the Master's voice has forever been silenced, or whether there is a way for it to make itself heard again.

Gaining methodological independence

The account of the gunshot in Telemark actualised a liminality inherent in the landscape representations of planning. From the narrator's point of view, neither a personal nor a professional integrity could be maintained within the conventional analytical approach that was expected of her. It became clear that what must be regarded as *data* in the study of landscapes cannot be merely the area in itself, nor its recountable elements, but rather the motives, processes and tools through which the image of an area, a landscape, is generated by an engaged agent. Using science's methodology for analysing landscapes and for the identification of *a character* in a tract of land hides the analysis as an act of gesturing, an act of showing (*action*). It disregards the landscape analyst's crucial responsibility to use his or her own judgement on how to present a landscape in a way that is relevant to the Convention's values as they may be applied in an actual situation. Any apparently value-free landscape analysis method risks neutralising (making invisible) the character of landscapes, rather than clarifying and enlightening an audience about their actual distinctiveness, in the present contexts of their emergence into appearance and as part of an utterance.

Contemporary pastoral analytical narration

The re-collection of a landscape is always bound to the conditions of its perception: unique or repeated, ordinary or extraordinary. The Telemark account can be looked upon as a typical landscape analysis situation, but one with an atypical ending. Precisely the ending highlights what often stays concealed in the typical cases, those with expected results: the fact that all landscape appreciation starts as subjectively experienced events and proceeds as reflection and judgement. The gunshot initiates a transformation in the analyst from emotional *labour,* first into a product of *work* (the account) and then into *action* (a reflection as it takes shape through the act of uttering a narrative of the event, a revised *work*). The realisation and communication of this process, the assembly of a landscape, therefore necessarily involves an element of narration.

In their comprehensive book on landscape narratives as design practices for telling stories, Matthew Potteiger and Jamie Purington look at landscape narratives as designating "the interplay and mutual relationship that develops between landscape and narrative" (Potteiger and Purinton, 1998:5). Places, they say, configure narratives, but narratives equally "play a critical role in making places" (Potteiger and Purinton, 1998:6). They present a list of nine types of landscape narratives, where all but one are ways in which narratives are inherent in *tangible* landscapes, landscape elements or landscape practices such as festivals or pilgrimages. In their type "narrative setting and topos", landscape is understood as part of a verbal/pictorial narrative in a way that is similar to our term *motif.* Interestingly, this type is exemplified with the *pastoral* topos, and the Telemark account's motif could aptly have served as an example of a narrative setting. None of their landscape narrative types, however, is purely verbal like the Telemark narrative. They do not acknowledge what we argue here, namely that the setting itself is narrated. Without the narrative there would be no landscape. As a version of pastoral poetics, a landscape accounts for those ways of knowing and acting that are exclusively provided by aesthetic engagement and experience in the land.

Additionally, the Telemark narrative is reflective in the sense that, in hindsight and on a more general level, it shows what insight may be obtained from looking at it as characterisable by its historicity. It testifies to *the time and circumstances of its emergence into appearance*; first when it was uttered in 1999 and then in this book. This is why the Telemark narrative is an *analytical* landscape narrative. An analytical landscape narrative discloses the important factors that lead to its exposure in this particular way. Instead of confirming one point of view, it opens up for others as well as later times to contest that point of view. Analytical landscapes must negotiate the interaction between convention and innovation through hermeneutic interpretation. They must also negotiate the distance between the analyst's and any potential reader's process of reflective perception.

A hermeneutics of landscape: convention and innovation

Discrepancy of vision can be highlighted as the fundamental problem of analysing landscapes in planning. As the pastoral idea has developed in a way that has led to its transformation into a variety of less and less recognisably pastoral landscapes, depending on the tools of their presentation, we seem to no longer be speaking about the same thing. The complexities of visual attention – the fact that Meliboeus and Tityrus, for instance, or the three people in Telemark share the same site and thus potential sights, but nevertheless not the same landscape – challenges the whole assumption that there could ever be something like a shareable landscape idea suitable as foundation for a publicly legitimate analysis.

Convention, on the one hand, is what makes us see the same object, a landscape for instance. As we saw in the Telemark narrative, the pastoral convention is what makes it possible for the site to be brought into the scene of the public realm as *landscape*. But on the other, it also comprises the tools and arguments with which we come to agree on really seeing the same object, for instance the act of photographing or a method of analysis. Thus, when part of a method, an analytical landscape narrative is bound to display a certain degree of conventionality. The conventionality in question, however, is not one that implies that landscapes are approached in the same way by all analysts alike; on the contrary, even a conventional way of seeing the same land is always a plurality of visions: every single observer approaches an environment from his or her personal viewpoint. The assertion of one's individuality and identity underlies the formation of individual images, both an analyst's as well as a reader's or listener's.

An approach to analysing landscapes must provide for a *plurality* of landscape visions to be able to be articulated and brought out into the public as different. It must offer a vital protection against the convention of seeing areas as landscapes becoming a stifling conformism. Such a conformism of landscape vision will eventually destroy the idea that there even is something real out there that it is possible to share with our fellow humans (Arendt, 1998:57–58):

> Under the conditions of a common world, reality is not guaranteed primarily by the "common nature" of all men who constitute it, but rather by the fact that, differences of position and the resulting variety of perspectives notwithstanding, everybody is always concerned with the same object. If the sameness of the object can no longer be discerned, no common nature of men, least of all the unnatural conformism of a mass society, can prevent the destruction of the common world, which is usually preceded by the destruction of the many aspects in which it presents itself to human plurality.

As we saw in the dialogue between Meliboeus and Tityrus in *Eclogue 1*, pastoral *discrepancy* lies in the separateness of the two speakers in their exchange about the circumstances by which they are both in some way affected as powerless in relation to a wider world. Tityrus is the conventional pragmatist who seeks a solution to his dilemmas within the apparatus of those in power. He has no need to see the world at reflective distance, in imagination. There is no need for an interpretation of his world as symbolic. What he needs is for his life to continue as it is; take a selfie from time to time and post it, or like B in the Telemark account, follow the prescribed way of carrying out a landscape analysis. Therefore, in Arendt's terms, convention is also what threatens the existence of the public realm: "It is quite conceivable that the modern age – which began with such an unprecedented and promising outburst of human activity – may end in the deadliest, most sterile passivity history has ever known" (Arendt, 1998:322). Meliboeus, on the other hand, who is in need of an understanding that can alleviate his pain, does not flee in silence but confronts his destiny with speech. The *action* of the analyst thus must be an attempt to avoid conventions and to rather trust in the convening of several perceiving eyes (Leach, 1974:47–48):

> In the final meeting of the pastoral world and the great world, a meeting that may be either a clash or a reconciliation, we come to understand the distance between the two regions, the ways in which each may reflect the other, and the possible interrelationships between the pastoral characters' experience and our own.

In order to avoid conformity and placidity, a landscape with its motifs, as objects of *work*, must be transformed into an instance of *action*. It must be analysed from the point of view of a current frame of action. A method of analysis requires an additional act of reflection from the analyst in order for his or her *subjective* image of the unity between humanity and nature to be brought into accordance with *motifs* delivered through a convention. The analyst must have a will to communicate, that is, to provide a space, in speech, where a landscape idea and an explicit ideal can be articulated and announced to an audience or readers.

Sharing visions in a polis of the eye

A landscape analyst's task is to turn an initial perceptive event into a commonly shareable analytical narrative: certain motifs are presented within an identified horizon of motion and a stated horizon of comprehension and thereby given a meaning. The *exchange* between expert and public, convention and innovation, as well as sensations and words, constitutes and legitimises a kind of insight. It is provided by what may be characterised as a *polis of the eye*, derived from Arendt's terminology. The analyst and the audience conjoin in a political *polis* based on verbal expressions about what they see and how they understand it: "To be political, to live in a polis, meant that everything was decided through words and persuasion and not through force and violence" (Arendt, 1998:26). Our idea of an analytical landscape narrative as activated in a polis of the eye constitutes a different rationale of legitimacy from the positivistic approaches that resort either to conventional static models or to psychological truths. We are looking for a landscape analysis method which can perform as politically as well as ontologically awareness-raising. In embedding the practice of analysing landscapes into an arena of public discourse, we may reinstate two major approaches to legitimising knowledge, both of which Lyotard (Lyotard, 1984), in his diagnosis of our postmodern computerised society, regretted as becoming outdated: we may read both a *political* and a *philosophical* approach to legitimising knowledge in the intentions of the European Landscape Convention. The politically emancipating contribution of raising landscape awareness can be identified in the Convention's belief in people's participation in landscape matters; the ontologically emancipating potential of raised awareness can be recognised in the Convention's belief in landscapes as a medium to enforce self-understanding. A *pastoral* and *analytically narrative* approach to analysing landscapes presents a way to combine these two legitimising strategies. Three aspects of the pastoral configuration of narratives are important in this respect.

The first aspect of pastoral configuration of narratives involves the public convening and speaking together of human figures on equal terms. This presence of plural voices produces a space for anyone to make their voice heard. Alpers has characterised pastoral literature as one where shepherds are part of a representative anecdote. They represent "those whose lives are determined by the actions of powerful men or by events and circumstances over which they have no control" (Alpers, 1996:162). Alpers' words summarise the performative effect of pastoral representation (Alpers, 1996:178):

> What is important for us is that the representational practices of pastoral – the forms of responsive dialogue, the way literary shepherds tend to present themselves as representative – lead to a sense of both sides being heard. Moreover, the tendency [...] to conclude eclogues on a note of suspended differences, is implicit in the pastoral ideal of human lives as mutually dependent and lived on common terms.

The Telemark episode, for instance, can also be seen as a classic case of representing different humans in a way that points to their common life terms on that day. Perceiving subjects, the onlookers no less than the looked-upon, risked being transformed into powerless objects, and with them, their landscapes into dead pictures. At the time of the event, the shooting may be conceptualised as an attempt at emancipation by the shooter, causing the two researchers to leave quickly. The man may have felt that the only way to maintain a certain degree of existential integrity was to stop any version of his home farm from being presented as a landscape (work) foreign to him, especially one based on a few "knowing" glances during an afternoon's visit. Or maybe his reaction was motivated by a local landscape heritage of violent revolt, as the shooting took place not far from a signpost commemorating a local farmers' (unsuccessful) uprising against the Danish king in the 17th century. His reaction was no verbal utterance, but still one that pertains to landscape narratives and landscape analysis. There is no polis in which to utter a landscape (*action*) for *any* of the protagonists of the story. Only through the pastoral analytical narrating (*action*) does the narrator recognise the man's reaction as a condition into which he was placed and which she shared when instructed to produce a landscape analysis according to a given but inappropriate procedure. This is an approach where the narrating voice of the analyst can be clearly identified and the landscape is kept alive as a medium of negotiation through the construction of the narrative itself.

A second aspect of the pastoral configuration of narratives is its construction of a confrontation of plural voices as a plot, an extraordinary event that calls for special attention. For an analysis to provide landscape awareness, we must therefore reverse the development whereby the poetic landscapes of Vergil, along their way from pastoral episodes in poetry via landscape pictures to the landscapes of contemporary planning, have been gradually emptied of imagined speaking and singing shepherds. An analytical narrative must trigger the readers as individuals, engaging them in their own sensing and making sense of the outside world. Although there is no singing contest in the Telemark narrative, no real exchange, we can still look at the story as one shepherd's song being offered to another. Even as an inner dialogue by the analyst him- or herself, the reflective narrative on the genesis of a landscape image is addressed, as *action*, to a potential reader whose life and environment it may affect, as well as to a greater world of things and their conventional apprehension. Alpers has explicitly pointed to the way the exchange between them is carried out in the literary pastoral tradition: "Literary shepherds often recall and sing for each other the songs of their masters and predecessors; so too the intertextuality of pastoral brings poet and reader(s) together in a literary space whose modulor [...] is the representative herdsman" (Alpers, 1996:81). The analytical narrative becomes a rhetorical tool. Its crucial legitimising factor is its capacity for presenting motifs as probable and meaningful. It does this by successfully appealing to imagination and critical observation, as we argued in chapter one.

A third aspect of the pastoral configuration of narratives is precisely that it creates a space between a horizon of motion and a horizon of comprehension, which Hunt has characterised as "that slippage from material thing to mental idea that lies at the heart of landscape experience" (Hunt, 2000:33). Words are inadequate, and a presented scene must always be visualised by a reader or listener who can "verify" it as a correct image. Crucially, analytical landscape narratives rely on and must make use of this basic inadequacy in order to re-present in ever new versions the connection between experience, understanding and knowledge.

The liminal space of an analytical narrative

In a planning situation, it is an attentive expert's role to suggest a translation of accidental perceptive events of everyday life in an area that helps them emerge into appearance as an exceptional vision, which is relevant according to an actual situation. In order for this to take place, the transition from a condition of *labour* to a condition of *work* to one of *action* must be made evident and traceable to the reader, as demonstrated in the analytical narrative of the gunshot event. A discrepancy must be introduced into the narrative between the everyday ordinariness of not seeing and the extraordinary act of seeing an area as landscape in the present circumstances of the analytical utterance. This means that there is no recourse to making extraordinary vision into an ordinary way of seeing. It is a matter of exposing through language the gap between the narrator's perspective at the time of constructing the analytical image and that of a reader at any present time. In the philosopher Jacques Rancière's words when referring to an art project called "I and us" in a deprived Parisian suburb, it is a matter of temporarily creating an aesthetic place for contemplation, away from the crowd and the dimension of social life, for "being together apart" (Rancière, 2009:53), thereby aesthetically laying grounds for re-creating a sense of community: "The construction of the solitary place aims at creating new forms of socialization and a new awareness of the capacity of anyone and everyone" (Rancière, 2009:59).

An analytical narrative must be put to use as both a poetic and rhetorical resource. As our environment is increasingly being programmed as instrumental in various ways, pastoral narratives should shape a space in which the diversity of more intimate and spontaneous connections between humankind as organic being and nature may find expression. In Rancière's words, it should encourage the "appropriation of the place of work and exploitation as the site of a free gaze. It does not involve an illusion but is a matter of shaping a new body and a new sensorium for oneself" (Rancière, 2009:71). It is to be made able to see the familiar with new eyes. It is precisely in such a space that the analyst and his or her audience might find what they have in common, albeit in different ways. It is by filling that space *for a very short moment* that both the analyst and his listeners may conjoin in a separately perceived but still shared landscape.

In the following chapter, we shall present attempts to implement and deepen the understanding of the terms and the narrative strategies that we have presented so far, incorporating them into the structure of conventional landscape analysis methods. Three examples will be presented where the analyst is clearly being heard voicing a pastoral ideal as it is brought into view by an actual landscape planning problem. Accordingly, three landscapes emerge into appearance and point to an answer to the planning task. In chapter five, then, we shall follow up a strategy of less fixed, more tentative and inviting ways of analysing areas as landscapes than is usual in planning today. We shall draft visions of everyday areas as *extraordinary* landscapes, exploring how these places may motivate a reflective attitude and the reader's capacity for environmental engagement. This is necessary at a time when the powerful motifs of maps and machine-mediated realities tend to overshadow the idea of landscape as symbolic of a humanity-nature unity.

References

Alpers, P. 1996. *What is pastoral?* Chicago, University of Chicago Press.

Andrews, M. 1999. *Landscape and Western art*, Oxford, Oxford University Press.

Arendt, H. 1998. *The human condition*, Chicago, University of Chicago Press.

Beardsley, M. C. & Beardsley, P. L. 1966. *Aesthetics from classical Greece to the present: a short history*, Tuscaloosa, University of Alabama Press.

Benediktsson, K. 2007. "Scenophobia", geography and the aesthetic politics of landscape. *Geografiska Annaler, Series B: Human Geography*, 89, 203–217.

Brunetta, G. & Voghera, A. 2008. Evaluating landscape for shared values: tools, principles, and methods. *Landscape Research*, 33, 71–87.

Clark, K. 1961. *Landscape into art*, London, Penguin.

Corner, J. 1990. A discourse on theory I: "Sounding the depths" – origins, theory, and representation. *Landscape Journal*, 9, 61–78.

Corner, J. 1991. A discourse on theory II: three tyrannies of contemporary theory and the alternative of hermeneutics. *Landscape Journal*, 10, 115–133.

Cosgrove, D. 1998. *Social formation and symbolic landscape*, Madison, University of Wisconsin Press.

Council of Europe. 2000. *European Landscape Convention*. Strasbourg, Council of Europe.

Czerniak, J. 1997. Challenging the pictorial: recent landscape practice. *Assemblage*, 34, 110–120.

Ellison, A. M. 2013. The suffocating embrace of landscape and the picturesque conditioning of ecology. *Landscape Journal*, 32, 79–94.

Geelmuyden, A. K. 1989. Økologisk arkitektur: en byggekultur på leting etter naturen – men hvilken natur? *Byggekunst*, 89, 237–242.

Geelmuyden, A. K. 1999. The landscape architect as landscape researcher: between empathy and reflective detachment in narratives of landscape – notes on the assessment of landscape values. *In*: Setten, G., Semb, T. & Torvik, R. (eds) *Shaping the land: proceedings of the Permanent European Conference for the Study of the Rural Landscape, 18th session in Røros and Trondheim, Norway, September 7th–11th 1998: volume 3: the future of the past*. Trondheim, Geografisk institutt, Universitetet i Trondheim.

Geelmuyden, A. K. & Fiskevold, M. 2016. Den europeiske landskapskonvensjonen: en pastorale for vår egen tid? *Nordisk Arkitekturforskning*, 28, 51–79.

Groh, R. & Groh, D. 1991. *Weltbild und Naturaneignung: zur Kulturgeschichte der Natur*, Frankfurt am Main, Suhrkamp.

Herrington, S. 2006. Framed again: the picturesque aesthetics of contemporary landscapes. *Landscape Journal*, 25, 22–37.

Hiltner, K. 2011. *What else is pastoral?: Renaissance literature and the environment*, Ithaca, Cornell University Press.

Hirsch, E. & O'hanlon, M. (eds). 1996. *The anthropology of landscape: perspectives on place and space*, Oxford, Clarendon Press.

Huggett, J. 2015. A manifesto for an introspective digital archaeology. *Open Archaeology*, 1(1): 86–95.

Hunt, J. D. 1992. *The pastoral landscape*, Washington, DC, National Gallery of Art.

Hunt, J. D. 2000. *Greater perfections: the practice of garden theory*, London, Thames & Hudson.

Hunt, J. D. & Willis, P. 1988. *The genius of the place: the English landscape garden 1620–1820*, Cambridge, MIT Press.

Leach, E. W. 1974. *Vergil's Eclogues: landscapes of experience*, Ithaca, Cornell University Press.

Lyotard, J.-F. 1984. *The postmodern condition: a report on knowledge*, Manchester, Manchester University Press.

Marburger, J. E. & Forman, R. T. T. 1997. Land mosaics. *Ecology*, 78, 642.

Marquard, O. 1981. *Abschied vom Prinzipiellen: philosophische Studien*, Stuttgart, Reclam.

Marx, L. 2000. *The machine in the garden: technology and the pastoral ideal in America*, Oxford, Oxford University Press.

Mcharg, I. L. 1992. *Design with nature*, New York, Wiley.

Meyer, E. K. 1998. Seized by sublime sentiments: between terra firma and terra incognita. *In*: Saunders, W. (ed.) *Richard Haag: Bloedel Reserve and Gas Works Park*. New York, Princeton Architectural Press with Harvard University Graduate School of Design.

Miljøverndepartementet. 1978. Forskrift om vern av Kolsås-Dælivann landskapsvernområde med plante- og fuglelivsfredninger og fire naturreservater i Bærum kommune, Akershus. *In*: Miljøverndepartementet (ed.) *FOR-1978-06-30-2*, Oslo, Miljøverndepartementet.

Panofsky, E. 1982. *Meaning in the visual arts*, Chicago, University of Chicago Press.

Panofsky, E. 1991. *Perspective as symbolic form*, New York, Zone Books.

Potteiger, M. & Purinton, J. 1998. *Landscape narratives: design practices for telling stories*, New York, Wiley.

Ramenofsky, A. F. & Steffen, A. 1998. *Unit issues in archaeology: measuring time, space, and material*, Salt Lake City, University of Utah Press.

Rancière, J. 2009. *The emancipated spectator*, London, Verso.

Relph, E. 1976. *Place and placelessness*, London, Pion.

Ritter, J. 1974. *Subjektivität: sechs Aufsätze*, Frankfurt, Suhrkamp.

Roger, A. 1997. *Court traité du paysage*, Mayenne, Gallimard.

Ruff, A. R. 2015. *Arcadian visions: pastoral influences on poetry, painting and the design of landscape*, Oxford, Windgather Press.

Seel, M. 1996. *Eine Ästhetik der Natur*, Frankfurt am Main, Suhrkamp.

Selman, P. H. 2006. *Planning at the landscape scale*, London, Routledge.

Straus, E. 1956. *Vom Sinn der Sinne: ein Beitrag zur Grundlegung der Psychologie*, Berlin, Springer.

Trepl, L. 2012. *Die Idee der Landschaft: eine Kulturgeschichte von der Aufklärung bis zur Ökologiebewegung,* Bielefeld, Transcript.

Tuan, Y.-F. 1977. *Space and place: the perspective of experience,* London, Edward Arnold.

Wellmer, A. 1985. *Zur Dialektik von Moderne und Postmoderne: Vernunftkritik nach Adorno,* Frankfurt am Main, Suhrkamp.

Wylie, J. 2007. *Landscape,* London, Routledge.

Chapter 4

Instances of pastoral motivation in contemporary landscape analytical practice

Creating landscapes within the analytical narrative's horizon of comprehension

Accepting the landscape analyst's influential *action* and ever-present commitment to explore and mediate the evolving world through analytical narratives brings us back to the pastoral motives presented in chapter one. We showed how the pastoral tradition, as a certain way of looking at humanity's physical environment, reflects a continuous contemplative attitude to human life according to three pastoral motives: the *emergence into appearance* of landscapes at a specific moment in time at which they are actualised as problematic, their existence within a diverse field of *discrepancies*, and finally their *emancipatory potential*.

The action of the landscape analyst supports the formation of new landscapes

The analysed landscape does not become part of reality before it is made visually accessible to a wider audience (Arendt, 1998:52):

> It means, first, that everything that appears in public can be seen and heard by everybody and has the widest possible publicity. For us, appearance – something that is being seen and heard by others as well as by ourselves – constitutes reality.

From our previous discussion, it follows that the reality of landscapes does not reside in land itself but is in need of the *action* of the analyst and the imagination of the utterance's addressees to become visible. Additionally, the *action* must be kept vital in the landscape analytical practice itself. In what follows we will demonstrate how the three fundamental pastoral motives, namely *appearance*, *discrepancy* and *emancipation*, could be used in three concrete cases to reformulate the technical analytical procedures which now pervade contemporary practices.

Using the momentum of its utterance, a landscape analysis can present landscapes with another approach to land than the habitual and conventional one. To the reader, the landscape which then can emerge into *appearance* for him or her is the landscape which is displayed *in* the analysis document or presentation. The landscape of the Norwegian World Heritage Site of Vegaøyan, for instance, is defined by the various narratives of the Unesco World Heritage Centre. Consequently, the showable motifs of the World Heritage landscape might differ from motifs of the same area that emanate from other ways of approaching the land. Landscape motifs have a synecdochic function in the narration of landscapes (Potteiger and Purinton, 1998). The realisation of the landscape is simply an outcome of anyone's ability to imagine the land with the World Heritage idea in mind. The emergence into appearance of the motifs of the analysis is an outcome of the World Heritage narrative's field of action and horizon.

The main topic of an analysis is the *discrepancy* which arises in the uttered landscape as it is explored in extension to, suspension or subversion of how land and landscapes are conceived in ordinary contemporary life. We shall demonstrate the *discrepancy* between a conceptual everyday landscape and the poetic landscape of the analyst in the case of Sarpefossen. In the utterance of this analytical narrative, the discrepancy of the narrated landscape lies in its presentation and articulation of visual arguments rather than in a listing of categorised visible land features. The *Et in Arcadia ego* of the landscape analysis is the threat of presenting a landscape merely as commodity, when instead of illuminating the encountered situation and thereby triggering and reinforcing imagination, the analysis' chosen words uncritically repeat well-known arguments or follow established analytical terms and procedures.

Finally, when articulated and introduced into the public discourse, an analysis may present alternative versions of the humanity-nature relationship which have *emancipating* powers. Landscape, as the cultural shaping of nature's events in perception, is uttered in words, made manifest in documents and prepared for dialogue and discourse. As Winsor Leach emphasises (Leach, 1974:109), the people and the scenes of the utterances should speak to the reader about a reality that is his or hers, in body, feelings and thoughts. As we shall see in the case of Storhei, the landscape is materialised in the dialogue and made present in an imagining convening. The inherent emancipative potential of the uttered motifs is picked up and enhanced by the analyst's motivation to make a hitherto absent/unacknowledged landscape appear within the everyday language of anyone interested. Transforming emotions and experiences into a clear and potent language fit for use in the public discourse should be the aim of the analysis' arguments.

Although the examples describe Norwegian cases, they all reflect major tendencies in international analytical practices: the World Heritage idea reflects the fact that the world to a large degree is influenced by global, economic and invisible decision makers; the idea of environmental impact assessments that manifests in the planning of Sarpefossen is motivated by the conviction that the effects of changes can be seen in advance; and the Storhei case is a version of the idea of justness and people's right to landscape.

Vegaøyan: exposing a World Heritage landscape through the lens of an analytical narrative

The analysis of Vegaøyan is a part of the idea of the Unesco World Heritage Centre

In 2004, the island of Vega, together with its surrounding archipelago, reefs and shallow channels, was designated a Unesco World Heritage Site (Figure 4.1). The main argument for its protected status, as articulated by the Unesco Nomination document, is the way in which Vegaøyan (Unesco, 2004):

> reflects the way generations of fishermen-farmers, over the past 1500 years, have maintained a sustainable living in an inhospitable seascape near the Arctic Circle, based on the now unique practice of eider down harvesting, and it also celebrates the contribution made by women to the eider down process.

Figure 4.1 Vega.

In other words, the site's outstanding universal values are linked to its status as a *cultural landscape*. The close link between vision, thought and language here served as the point of departure for a further elaboration in a landscape analysis which was carried out during the summer of 2016. The foundation Verdensarv Vegaøyan commissioned Sweco, an interdisciplinary consultancy enterprise, to carry out the analysis with specific focus on whether modern fish-farming activities were in line with the World Heritage protection intentions (Fiskevold, 2016b). In this case, seeing the area as a cultural landscape therefore meant that an analysis had to make a landscape emerge into appearance within the Unesco statutes' horizon of comprehension. The report concluded that modern fish farms were not compatible with the outstanding values of the World Heritage Site.

Appearance, as it is evoked by the analysis, is a collective event, even though it is always perceived through subjective attention to some objective materiality. The analysis of the visual character of the World Heritage landscape thus demonstrates how a landscape is always attached to the framing horizon of a larger narrative and an idea which assembles and combines elements of the land into visible motifs, potential images offered to the reader's imagination. In the case of Vegaøyan, the Unesco World Heritage Centre itself provides a certain version of the pastoral culture of vision. Although the narrated image "reflect[s] the way generations of fishermen/ farmers have [...] maintained a sustainable living in an inhospitable seascape" (Unesco, 2004), the analysis is also shaped by the history of the World Heritage Centre itself. In order both to analyse the visual character and to assess whether contemporary aquaculture industry enhances or weakens the visual character of the World Heritage landscape, one has to know how Unesco have articulated and interpreted *cultural* landscapes, that is, *their* convention of seeing the world as landscape.

Conceiving an image of the World Heritage landscape means bringing into play a number of previous narratives. First of all, our view is framed by what it means to perceive it as a *cultural landscape*. According to Unesco's *Operational Guidelines* (Unesco World Heritage, 2008:§47):

> [Cultural landscapes] are cultural properties and represent the "combined works of nature and of man" designated in Article 1 of the [Landscape] Convention. They are illustrative of the evolution of human society and settlement over time, under the influence of the physical constraints and/or opportunities presented by their natural environment and of successive social, economic and cultural forces, both external and internal.

Additionally, Vegaøyan is defined as an organically evolved landscape: "a continuing landscape is one which retains an active social role in contemporary society closely associated with the traditional way of life, and in which the evolutionary process is still in progress" (Unesco World Heritage, 2008:Annex III). All these definitions and paragraphs mean that the World Heritage landscape in Vegaøyan is understood as the visible reflection of a human attitude towards nature which has evolved over time and which is still practised there.

Secondly, the construction of the visual World Heritage character of Vegaøyan was further assisted by investigating earlier controversies over other World Heritage Sites where visual issues had been at stake. In the Loire Valley (2000), for instance, the site of a nuclear power station was excluded from the World Heritage Site. In the Elbe Valley (2004–2009), more dramatically, the entire site was removed from Unesco's World Heritage List due to the building of a four-lane bridge in the heart of the designated cultural landscape.

Finally, the construction of the visual World Heritage character of Vegaøyan was based on issues regarding the Vegaøyan site itself. According to the designation document, the site's *authenticity* is tied to human subsistence on the shelf, while its *integrity* means that all the characteristic elements in the cultural landscape of the "strandflat" (coastal brim) are represented. Even more cues to characterisation had been given during the process of defining a limit to the site, in that the process explicitly excluded a radio mast as well as all areas on Vega Island where new development had been endorsed by municipal plans. Furthermore, the relation between fish-farming and the World Heritage landscape was touched upon, but not elaborated or thoroughly discussed following the designation: neither in strategic coastal plans, in the assessments for environmental zoning, nor in any aquaculture licensing processes. It was plainly stated that no contradiction existed between the two land use approaches within the borders of the World Heritage Site.

Motifs of the World Heritage landscape

Whereas the analyst's image formation initially will depart from the basic experiences that make up human existence on the shelf, such as for instance the obvious importance of the weather for life on the archipelago, this shared horizon will gradually be transposed into an objectively accessible motif when re-presented in an analysis. In the case of Vegaøyan, this transformation of a common-*sense* landscape took place when a *conceptual* common ground was established by combining the World Heritage principles, earlier site controversies and site-specific practices. Three analytical concepts were extracted from the narratives of the World Heritage Centre in order be able to link it visually to the area's appearance as landscape: *practice, place* and *continuity*. Although this conceptual step was carried out by the analyst, the point of departure was delivered by narratives beyond the analyst's influence. Thus, the identification of landscape character was still framed by a shared knowledge and experience base, but the essential keywords were extracted from the Unesco narrative. *Practice* denoted the visual character which resulted exclusively from the inhabitants' customary use of the natural resources in the area. *Place* denoted the non-human visual scene which surrounded life on the shelf, such as journeying between islands and mainland, and continuous adjustment to the seasons or other shifting conditions. *Continuity* denoted the degree to which the coherence of practice and place still prevailed and left visual traces in the area.

In a last analytical step, the analytical concepts of *practice*, *place* and *continuity*, as they symbolically appeared through the concrete features in the area, led to the articulation of four fundamental motifs, visually concretising the character of the World Heritage landscape (Figure 4.1):

(1) Vegaøyan is situated on the shelf between the ocean and the inland mountain ridge, which visually delimits the area to the north, south and east. These features constitute the motif of a landscape situated between the infinity of ocean and the wall of the mountains.

(2) The tide and the shallow waters contribute to an ever-changing and cyclical revealing and concealing of land and sea. This gave material support to a motif of constant change and reappearance of sea surface and land surface.

(3) Even in the parts close to the mainland, the sight of the many reefs appearing as narrow black ribbons visually suggests the presence of the ocean beyond, thereby supporting a motif of contrast between imagined infinity and tangible horizon.

(4) Life on the edge shows itself in the way the settlements either are protected from the ocean by land forms or distinctly stand out on the low horizon. Some places offer protection, while in other places human settlements are left exposed to the forces of water and air. The different configurations constitute different ocean settlement motifs, which further underscore the visual character of the World Heritage landscape.

The visual character of the World Heritage landscape, as exposed in these motifs, is certainly not a property of the land, but an outcome of human seeing, reflection and communication. When part of an analysis that is an argumentative utterance, a motif always has an aim and a direction. The delivered analysis of the World Heritage landscape is both derived from and directed towards the general narratives of the Unesco World Heritage Centre as well as its specific narrative of the Vegaøyan site. The surface of the earth must be left behind when the task is to re-present its visual appearance through a text, a map or an illustration, and to point at some referent, name or location. The analysis does not represent past events of experience, but rather is the result of an interpretation and judgement that was prepared but not completed on site. In Arendt's words (Arendt, 1978:133):

The meaning of what actually happens and appears while it is happening is revealed when it has disappeared; remembrance, by which you make present to your mind what actually is absent and past, reveals the meaning in the form of a story.

A motif does not duplicate the land; nor is it, however, independent of the land. Even when a photographic motif is perceived at the same spot and with the same angle of view as the photographer once beheld it, seeing the land with the image of the photographic motif in mind means that the perception is heavily influenced by the idea that is encompassed in the seen and re-viewed motif.

Imagination as the subjective entrance to a landscape

Having shown how constructed motifs work as tiny bridges between experiences in a site and the analyst's utterance about it, the appearance of the World Heritage landscape of Vegaøyan is still dependent on subjective imagination for its emergence into appearance as subjective landscape image. The performance of imagination is an individual act of perception. Arendt describes imagination accurately as a shift from the visible materiality of the world into an invisible image of the world (Arendt, 1978:75–76):

Every mental act rests on the mind's faculty of having present to itself what is absent from the senses. Re-presentation, making present what is actually absent, is the mind's unique gift, and since our whole mental terminology is based on metaphors drawn from vision's experience, this gift is called *imagination*, defined by Kant as "the faculty of intuition even without the presence of the object".

In February 2017 a group of experts, politicians and bureaucrats gathered in Bodø. The occasion for the gathering was a Unesco advisory mission which was motivated by some controversies between the aquaculture industry, the area's visual character and the World Heritage status of the archipelago. The meeting addressed the issue of heritage, aquaculture and sustainability. Different positions were presented, discussed and reported. Statistics, verbal arguments, maps and photographs were highlighted to the attentive audience. However, the sound of a voice alone cannot develop a meaningful image of a randomly selected piece of land. As Arendt stresses, imagination is the decisive faculty which prepares material experiences for mindful elaboration and evaluation (Arendt, 1978:77):

Imagination, therefore, which transforms a visible object into an invisible image, fit to be stored in the mind, is the condition *sine qua non* for providing the mind with suitable thought-objects; but these thought-objects come into being only when the mind actively and deliberately remembers, recollects and selects from the store-house of memory whatever arouses its interest sufficiently to induce concentration.

Imagination could be regarded as an essential component in the process of *theoria* or contemplation, the *vita contemplativa*, which Gadamer describes as a communion with the appearing phenomenon (Gadamer, 2010:115) or a *Mitspielen,* a participating presence with the work of art (Gadamer, 1977:31). Although the image itself is not shared, the conviction of similarity is shared. Herein lies its rhetorical power as argument and as transmitter of knowledge about the world.

Sarpefossen: extracting a poetic landscape from an ordinary area

Some years ago, a landscape analysis was carried out as part of an investigation of the possibility of constructing a new road bridge at Sarpefossen, the area around a large waterfall on Norway's largest river, Glomma. The site was in Sarpsborg, a town some 150 km south-east of Oslo. Although the project was terminated before any conclusion was reached, the case inspired the development of an alternative to the conventionally used methods (Fiskevold, 2016c). Approaching a task like that means being directly engaged in pastoral *discrepancy.* As the outcome of a journey as well as of cultural narratives in an area, landscape is an instantaneous sensation and an object of experience and thought, both at the same time. When they are themselves presented as analytical narratives, however, landscapes *appear* as objects of language and memory. Although any landscape is influenced by and essentially dependent on material experiences, the challenge for the analyst, first of all, is how to release the poetic potential inherent in the act of narrating. In order to do this, he or she has to rely on his or her own skills to assemble all relevant sources and avoid conventional and maybe already outdated narratives. Additionally, the analyst has to pay close attention to the expected *form* of the analysis. In the case of Sarpefossen, for example, the analysis was expected to be carried out following a specific assessment method, its procedure and terminology dramatically narrowing down the analyst's field of action. In the landscape analyst's articulation of an analytical narrative, therefore, the discrepancy between positive and negative ideals is located first and foremost in the tension between different approaches to the analytical process.

Creating a landscape metaphor in extension of a well-known horizon of comprehension

An analysis threatens to tear to pieces the complex synthetic unity implied by the idea of landscape, and risks constructing a motif which mediates only a very limited or even false image of the area as landscape. Many current methods of landscape analysis reveal a view of the world as a duality made up of an external reality and a representation of that reality. In the pastoral tradition, on the other hand, the world is a human-made and ordered construction which consists of material and immaterial entities. Exposing landscapes through analytical narratives means taking advantage both of well-known positive and less-known negative ideals, which together inform the utterance of a landscape image. An analytical narrative offers the analyst an opportunity to articulate a contemporary landscape in relation to, but still independently of the field of action afforded by mainstream thought, methodology and categories.

Consequently, a planning task like that in Sarpsborg means working within horizons provided by the analysis *as text*. As text, the analytical narrative combines several horizons into one account. Different motifs are combined into a new landscape. The plurality and complexity of horizons is described by Gérard Genette in his *Narrative discourse* from 1972. The literary scholar Terry Eagleton summarises the main arguments of Genette's book in the following way (Eagleton, 2008:91):

> [Genette...] draws on a distinction in narrative between *récit*, by which he means the actual order of events in the text; *histoire*, which is the sequence in which those events "actually" occurred, as we can infer this from the text, and *narration*, which concerns the act of narrating itself.

Following Genette, we recognise the presented horizon of the analysed landscape, such as can be inferred from the landscape analysis at Sarpefossen, in the term *récit*. The horizon of the recollected perception of land, such as the account of the journey around Sarpefossen or the site's historical development, is its *histoire*. The contribution of the *récit* is to hide the discontinuity of the *histoire*. Finally, *narration* is the act of the analyst who compounds of all these horizons.

The analyst must seize the opportunity to create new landscapes by introducing into an analytical narrative a *récit* which reorders the *histoire*'s order of land appearances through his or her narration. The analytical narrative has the powers to combine the different horizons into one line of argumentation, an articulated guide to seeing, which will lead the reader to imagine the represented tract of land as a certain landscape. In this move, the ordinary horizon of comprehension is expanded by the extraordinary horizon of the analytical narrative. It is a reordering of material and immaterial experiences, which is then distributed onto the land by means of other media, such as names and maps. Accordingly, narrating a landscape means a re-localisation, a re-temporalisation and a re-conceptualisation of land features in a de-sensed image. In this re-constructive act, motifs from different places and eras are combined to give the proposed image a comprehensible shape. Through metaphorical use, concrete experiences and visible features become literary motifs to re-present invisible images, in Arendt's words, "turning the mind back to the sensory world in order to illuminate the mind's non-sensory experiences for which there are no words in any language" (Arendt, 1978:106).

Crossing the bridge at Sarpefossen, for example, gazing at the masses of water pouring through the narrow rift in the bedrock, one might imaginatively trace the river's way back to its sources, envisioning the snow-covered mountains and forested valleys of south-eastern Norway and the water's eroding work there since the last ice age (Figure 4.2). One might reiterate the river's history as transport artery for logs, or see this location as the water's final leap down to the fjord where lumber could be shipped off to central Europe or some other, much closer paper factory. Thus, one would gain full comprehension of the reasons for the existence of Sarpsborg as a town, for its layout and architecture. The transition between horizons of motion and comprehension and the resulting array of motifs performs a metaphorical transmission: the image of the water masses of Sarpefossen, for instance, may give impetus for a diversity of landscape motifs in a site, when the image is used to re-collect the history of land and people in an analytical narrative. In a similar way, a theme map of Sarpefossen can be used metaphorically to give meaning to the landform of the area, illuminating the two levels upstream and downstream of the waterfall (Figure 4.3). The map

Figure 4.2 Sarpefossen.

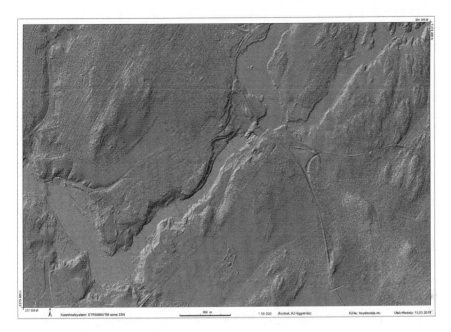

Figure 4.3 Map of Sarpefossen.

sheet itself acts as a metaphor, transferring a potentially sensed journey into the shades and colours on a screen or a piece of paper. The ensuing land-scape image does not emerge from the face of the land, then, but from the map's picture.

Creating landscape motifs through argumentation

The metaphorical design of analytical narratives turns them into a tool to transfer a concept of landscape into specific features and sites in an area (Figure 4.4). In a coherent line of argumentation, the *action* of the analyst joins up with the *work* (the analytical narrative), adding immaterial values to material features and sites. Visible motifs, like the photograph and theme map of Sarpefossen, stay in the foreground of this symbolic transaction, whereas ideas such as the pastoral humanity-nature unity are background components of the metaphorical act. The conventional methodological approach to landscape analysis tends to start with types of motifs without any clear conceptual base. The method's argumentative procedures thereby lose aim and direction, and the method is simultaneously turned into a static model for unreflected replication. Rather, what an analytical narrative should encourage is a version of the traditional way of seeing an area's land-scape character in a way that responds to the world of today. Importantly,

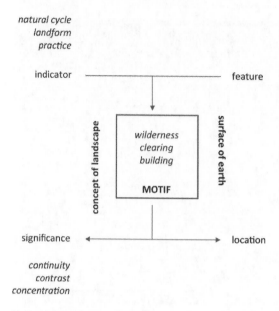

Figure 4.4 Landscape formation extended with analytical terminology. The "input" is features of the land perceived as indicators of a concept. The product is a motif. The "output" is the significance and location of the motif.

though, the image's conceptual components are aspects of an embracing idea. They must not be treated literally as entities in their own right.

Indicators of pastoral landscapes must be derived from the ideal of humanity-nature unity, such as for instance the evidences of nature's *cycles*, present *landform* and human land *practices*. These render the unity between humanity and nature visible and serve to re-present the idea of landscape. Through the term *natural cycle*, an engagement with and awareness of the ephemeral, never-ending processes of nature may be evoked by pointing to selected features in the city centre of Sarpsborg, at the manor of Hafslund or even in the industrial plant of Borregård. It could be the variations of light and shade or of seasons and weather, it could be animal life and human behaviour. One could point out how these forces are manifest in vegetation, water and the built environment. Through the term *landform*, an engagement with and awareness of the ever-continuing shape of the earth's surface may be evoked by pointing at the gradual or abrupt land rises and falls along the natural river gorge, the constructed power station's location in relation to these, as well as the remnants of a landslide which swept large parts of the medieval town into the river several hundred years ago. Through the term human *practice*, an engagement with and awareness of the invisible human attitude towards nature may be evoked by pointing to how the manor of

Hafslund and its surrounding park underline the land ridge called Raet. In a nature reserve nearby, the surface of the earth reveals itself as a product of another human practice: human engagement in enhancing environmental diversity.

Scanning the surface of the earth surrounding Sarpefossen, using *natural cycle*, *landform* and *practice* as conceptual indicators, the analyst's aim is to articulate visible motifs with which to make the area emerge into appearance as landscape, and thereby evoke awareness of it. These motifs occur as the visible outcome of human reflection related to land, as they can be partly extracted from features in the area that are influenced by human evaluation and choice. Following Arendt's three modes of human activity – *labour*, *work* and *action* – and the corresponding typology of organic, material and articulated landscapes, we can also talk about characterising types of motifs: *wilderness*, *clearing* and *building*. Designating an area as *wilderness* landscape, for instance, means that the area makes it possible to sense oneself as in a state of *labour* through the body's motion. A *clearing* area indicates an area which makes it possible to perceive human work on and *with* nature through the character of the land. Lastly, a *building* area is an area which enables us to perceive deliberate human transformation of nature as it stands out as different relative to an idea of humanity-nature unity.

Using the presence or absence of human intervention as a methodologically guiding idea, the canyon below Sarpefossen (the waterfall) could be identified as a landscape of *wilderness* due to its steep ridges and large precipitous flow of water. The *wilderness* motif provides the individual with the image of a materiality which to a large extent is unaltered by human intervention.

Simultaneously, the hydropower station built into Sarpefossen appears as an instance of the *building* motif due to the entire transformation of the riverbed into a human artefact. A *building* motif can also be perceived in the adjacent industrial complex of Borregård as well as in the manor and landscape park of Hafslund. Regardless of building material, be it concrete or lawn, the human *building* motif becomes visible and dominant in areas where humans have totally co-opted the natural cycle into their practices. Additionally, the motif is recognisable where the landform is being exclusively adapted to some kind of human programme.

Further upstream, on either side of the river, there are different areas which can be categorised as belonging to the *clearing* motif. The most obvious are the agricultural fields, but the woods used for timber production, the large storage areas of the timber processing industry and the car parks for the workers also belong here. The *clearing* motif becomes visible in areas where humans cultivate and modify nature, thereby leaving a landform that is heavily influenced by human activity. The *clearing* motif provides the individual with an image of the surface of the earth where humans negotiate with nature.

It is the landscape analyst who, in a stepwise conceptual assessment, assembles and selects the land features which can be grouped into the visible motifs of *building, clearing* and *wilderness*. It is also the analyst who initiates the next step in the process. It is *his* or *her* own decision, then, to now distribute the selected and assembled features as motifs into identifiable spatial *landscape areas*. Translating a visible motif into a concrete physical location implies both a selection of *scale* and an interpretation of *situation*. The visibility of *wilderness* is apparent in areas whose character is influenced by the labour of nature, where the landform generally has remained unaltered and where there are few visible traces of cultural practices. As such, depending on the scale, this motif could be apprehended both in the distant mountains of the river's large catchment area and in the ditches along the road leading to Sarpefossen bridge. The motifs of *clearing* and *building* show a similar proliferation regarding scale. The simple stone tumulus guiding the mountain hiker is as much an instance of *building* as the bridge construction over Sarpefossen. As objects of sight they both fill the viewshed of the observer, but as features located in the land, they nevertheless influence the visual character of the land differently. A similar decision of landscape characterisation must be carried out when a site, as occasionally happens, appears differently at different times. The *building* motif as located in the hydropower station's concrete walls, terraces and bridges, for instance, can be attributed to the *wilderness* motif when huge amounts of water from melting snow the mountains in southern Norway surge through the narrow opening in the cliff (see Figure 4.2).

The landscape analysis of Sarpefossen presents the area as a contemporary pastoral landscape where the motifs of *building, clearing* and *wilderness* make up its layout and visualise its character. However, landscape assessments most often also conclude with an evaluation of the analytically identified landscape. The *building* motif of the hydropower station and the manor park of Hafslund both demonstrate human interventions in the surface of the earth, but their significance or value as a landscape based on the landscape pastoral idea of humanity-nature unity is nevertheless not necessarily the same.

In the above-mentioned landscape analysis, the degree of natural integrity in the Sarpefossen area was articulated in terms of *continuity, contrast* and *concentration*. Using these terms to describe the significance of the hydropower station, we find a *concentration* of built constructions which usually disrupt the *continuity* of the stream, thereby weakening the visual presence of the water's free natural force. But simultaneously, the bare rocks surrounded by the concrete walls, buildings and terraces of the power station visually offer a *contrast* to landforms which, still visually, reveal the original bedrock of the land ridge *Raet*. The sight of the rock makes it easy to imaginatively follow the *continuation* of the land formation *Raet* and its genesis through sedimentation, over 10,000 years ago. The *continuity* in time can equally be followed in space. Moving westwards, the formation of *Raet* makes up the ground of the modern city centre of Sarpsborg. Its main street and plaza are situated on the top of the ridge, with its street grid sloping down in opposite directions. Moving eastwards, the *continuation* of *Raet* can be followed through to the manor of Hafslund, appearing as both an extension of the ridge (*concentration*) and as a built *contrast* to it, thereby causing the landform to significantly emerge into appearance. In addition, the garden of Hafslund visually represents the idea of humanity-nature unity which assembles any type of landscape into a *concentrated* image of the interplay of natural cycles, landform and human practices. In the rich agricultural areas surrounding the town, motifs provided by the cycle of the year offer a number of diverse *contrasts*: from the snow-covered white fields in winter, to the dark brown ones in autumn and spring, and the green and yellow stretches of grain in summer.

Imagination mediates between everyday and poetic landscapes

Addressed to a wider audience, the utterance of the analytical narrative is also an opportunity to take advantage of the discrepancy between a conventionally perceived everyday landscape and an analyst's poetically interpreted landscape. No analytical narrative should passively record conventional opinions about the land, but it should rather engage its audience by stimulating individuals' imaginative capacities. Pastoral motivation may cause anyone to imaginatively interpret the appearance of the earth as an instance of the unity between humanity and nature. In this relation, nature is an ongoing force, indifferent to human struggles, hopes, morals and ideas of justice. Consequently, modernity's landscape pastoral attitude implies that the analyst must introduce the ideal of a unity between humanity and nature as recognisable within everyday human activity. The analyst constructs an imaginative model of this unity, aiming to articulate a stance in a decision-making process (*action*). The modelled image is mediated as the analysed landscape, and should be formulated so as to reach the imagination of a motivated reader or listener. The aim of this practice is to evoke and support the imaginative capacities in a broader audience. Thus the vitality of the image depends on the imaginative capacity of the observer to tap into the stories, allegories and images which are or can be culturally attached to land.

Subjective emancipation: translating awareness into identity

In an increasingly globalised world, the plurality of horizons operating in the same area stresses the importance of knowing one's own landscape and having the skill to articulate it as a potentially decisive voice in a discourse of contradictory intentions. In recent years, there have been many debates on proposed wind turbine plants in Norway. In one of these cases, Storhei, in the small municipality of Birkenes in the southern part of Norway, one of us had the chance to participate both as a professional analyst and as a researcher (Fiskevold, 2016a). The search for professional ways to articulate landscape as "common good" brought with it the realisation of one aspect of the emancipatory potential of landscape analyses: simply to introduce a new horizon of meaning to local people's land perception and confront their habitual horizon.

Entering the horizon of a landscape analysis through the action of the analyst

E.ON, one of the world's largest investor-owned power and gas companies, covers the Nordic region from its regional office in the southern Swedish town of Malmö. On commission from E.ON, the Norwegian branch of the Swedish engineering company Sweco has identified the available wind resources of large parts of the Norwegian territory. The overall aim of this was to obtain a production licence for wind power from the Norwegian Water Resources and Energy Directorate. In the small municipality of Birkenes, the initiative provoked an intense debate. Some supported the transformation of the area, leaning on financial arguments. Others, a diverse group of landowners and land users organised in the local initiative group Motvind (a play on words, literally meaning "headwind"), emphasised the area's unique wilderness character. The absence of technical infrastructure in the area simply exposed the land as a landscape that they felt was a fundamental aspect of their livelihood and a substantial part of their identity.

The split between insiders and outsiders of landscape in the Storhei discourse cannot be drawn between inhabitants of the area and external interests. In this case as well as in the Vegaøyan case, the demarcation line between those who perceive the contested area as a landscape and those who perceive it as a means to some financial, political or bureaucratic end follows the horizon of the pastoral landscape idea. But even for those who literally and metaphorically *inhabit* the land as landscape, their long-practised but yet unarticulated landscape needs the horizon of comprehension of an analytical narrative in order to be able to enter the discursive arena. Arguments concerning landscape, identity, and social and individual well-being have to find their way into the legal, political and commercial mechanisms, procedures, regulations and institutions. These driving forces and their horizons of comprehension constitute an arena which has been established and designed by those already adapted and well integrated to the planning discourse.

A landscape analysis is an utterance in the polis of *public* planning and thus addressed to a particular audience. It is an utterance based on a landscape idea which can be identified as pastoral in a very conventional pictorial sense

(Geelmuyden and Fiskevold, 2016), and it is articulated as a *method* with a standardised procedure and fixed landscape indicators. In Storhei as well as in the Sarpefossen case, landscape analyses were professionally carried out according to a standard environmental impact assessment method developed by the Norwegian Road Department (Statens vegvesen, 2014). Fiskevold has demonstrated how the widespread use of this methodological approach is due to the fact that it is designed primarily for a certain kind of *efficiency* (Fiskevold, 2011). The method is meant to lead to results that are comparable across disciplines or professional perspectives, to knowledge which can be operationalised instantly as a numerically expressed assessment of impact. Furthermore, the method is meant to be useful on any planning scale, and finally, its procedure is mandatory, meaning that it must be followed regardless of situation. In short, the method neatly suits the idea that knowledge is valuable when it enhances productive efficiency (Lyotard, 1984:11). When embraced by this horizon of comprehension, landscape is primarily understood as a phenomenon which can be explained and presented as object, by a value-free step-by-step procedure that minimises the engagement of the individual.

To a large degree, this idea of efficiency determines the outcome of the analysis. This also means, however, that the expert is prevented from fully appreciating and operationalising the landscape concept of the European Landscape Convention. In landscape analysis commissions like that in Storhei, the expert is limited to habitual reiteration of the prescriptions given in the assessment programme. Accepting this mandate, he or she effectively must ward off the multiple and diverse possible perceptions of the area's visible and experienced characteristics, which may provide foundations for social and individual well-being. The locals at Storhei, who were apparently engaged and aware of the land's potential as landscape, seemed to lack practice in giving their bodily experiences linguistic form and were ignorant of the cultural tradition of landscape appreciation. They overlooked the potential it held for strong arguments for their cause, and eagerly produced a rich array of arguments which, however, lacked the support of an appropriate guiding idea. In this situation, a research project initiated by Fiskevold provided a possibility to introduce the landscape pastoral idea in which, as became clear, the members of Motvind as well as the expert could take part. Additionally, the project offered an occasion to test a way of substantiating landscape as *common good* on the stage of public governance and decision-making.

Materialising pastoral landscape motifs through dialogue

Unlike most professional projects, where landscape motifs are developed based primarily on a predefined expert approach, the case of Storhei offered an alternative way to materialise landscape motifs of the area. The professional approach of an expert and the engagement of the Motvind members made it possible to have a constructive exchange of images and to develop arguments. In an expert-driven dialogue, landscape motifs were identified and articulated. The dialogue was carried out in both written and oral media. In addition to mail correspondence involving map-drawing and topic-related questions, a field trip in the area was suggested as part of the exploration. Introducing a dialogue with the Motvind members was a way of releasing mere impressions and convictions into deliberate utterances and text. In the linguistic interplay between human intentions and natural appearances, a complex and permanent landscape emerged, which gained its substance from past and current material practices, cultural narratives, individual attention, and verbal articulation and communication. Gradually, the correspondence and discussions produced visible outcomes in the form of pastoral landscape motifs of the land. Some of them are described in the following.

During the field trip, the walking frequently interrupted the talking, but talking equally often continued during walking. The exchange between words and ground, mediated through the moving bodies and the searching and assembling eyes, kept the trip participants' attention tied to the interplay of apprehensions and motifs. Our searching eyes spotted places at varying distances from the path. Introducing a scholarly horizon to the group, German-American psychologist Erwin Straus' term *die Ferne* ("that which is situated far away", our translation) was a way of translating the vague but crucial apprehension of the land through the receiving but not yet conceiving act of bodily movement (Straus, 1956:408). Crossing valleys, moors, ice-covered lakes or small hills, body and eye together constitute a dynamic unity which opens up for site-specific perceptions. In this organic act, described by Straus as *ein Mit-Werden* (Straus, 1956:409), a "co-becoming", the individual contributes with its body, and the area with its surface. The members of Motvind repeatedly mentioned this unique attraction of the Storhei area. Seemingly inexpressible with words, the experience of knowing the area, involving the body's motion, the sensed site and the visual intake of close and distant features, could be grasped by the term *die Ferne*, and it gradually became part of an analytical (through the term) landscape (through the awareness) pastoral narrative (through the dialogue).

Another landscape motif, the ruins of the old hay barn at Orreleiksheia, emerged into appearance as an outcome of the Motvind members' knowledge of its significance in former agricultural practices and the expert's knowledge of the term *chronotope*, first introduced by the Russian literary scholar Mikhail Bakhtin (Bakhtin, 2006). The Motvind members visualised the moor harvest as one of the most important stories about the area. The grass of the moors was harvested, barns were built for both storage and temporary accommodation, and in the winter season the hay crop was transported home. The materialisation of the motif thus took place just as

Bakhtin has described the formation of a chronotope, a fusion of time and space, where time "thickens, takes on flesh, becomes artistically visible; likewise, space becomes charged and responsive to the movements of space, plot and history" (Bakhtin, 2006:84). The continuity of walking and talking, of gesturing towards the land or pausing in the conversation, gradually increased the presence of landscape motifs in the area, as well as the group's awareness of the area's landscape potential. Experience and narrative did not make one another superfluous, but complemented and supplemented one another. With each new experiential event, a larger potential of the narrative was disclosed, and vice versa. New knowledge affected the whole group, both expert and Motvind members. As an outcome of the moving body and the searching eye, landscape motifs materialised and eventually expanded the horizon of the narrative.

Imaginative convening enacted through words

Much of the emancipatory power of an analytical narrative lies in the fact that it presents a subjectively perceived image that is temporarily released from societal codes. As an explanation proposed by the expert, an *action* on his or her part, the valued interaction of bodily experience and reflexive thought that took place in Storhei made it possible to obtain independence from the otherwise prevailing idea of nature as well regulated and technically controlled. As we saw in chapter three, theorists of modernity such as Ritter and Clark hold that landscape has its conceptual roots in the pastoral codification of nature. Its essence is the aesthetic enjoyment of nature's phenomena and processes when undisturbed by human regulation (Ritter, 1974:7; Clark, 1961) and the alternative that this way of seeing provides to everyday life's routines and obligations. Perceived as landscape, the Storhei area offers the possibility of a unique form of bodily movement, realisable as such through the accentuating exception from everyday mobility, whether that of a car driver or that of a pedestrian confined to paved streets or roads (Figure 4.5). At the same time, the area offers traces of earlier ways of life, presenting themselves as an imaginative supplement to contemporary practices and conceptions. Accordingly, the meaning of the Storhei landscape could be said to reside in the interplay between modified and unmodified materiality, regulated and unregulated activity, conceptualised and still unconceptualised reality. Areas like Storhei, seen as landscapes, offer aesthetic alternatives to seeing nature in terms of science, economic profit or bureaucratic procedures, such as in the form of a wind power development or methods for assessing landscape values in the area. The possibility to experience and visualise the land as landscape without the guidelines of a prescribed route or method of assessment is what makes up the revealing act of seeing and the emancipating potential of realising landscape motifs. Following this landscape approach, areas like Storhei can be regarded as a

Figure 4.5 Walking on thin ice in the landscape of Storhei.

still unrealised potential within the known world. Such areas are a standing reserve of potential experiences and image formations.

While we were walking and talking in Storhei, sights and knowledge came together in a process where personal and cultural histories were given visible form. Ties of belonging between the area and the individual were shaped. The individual perceiver contributed with his or her looking and seeing, society with its narratives. Through this activity, narratives were transferred to sites in the area. In a site-specific context, personal experiences were "added" to the ground. Both the place and the individual gained an interrelated but still separate character, as landscape and individual. Words projected the sight of the individual to distant and unknown places in the area, as verbally expressed perceptions and images were left open to everyone else's interpretative skills. The shared acts of speaking and visualising were carried out as a coming together within images that we previously termed *a polis of the eye*. Visualisation, in itself internal to an individual mind, needs to be thought and uttered in words to become visible as a motif, as a piece of *work*. Though individually uttered, the proposed sights at Storhei were verified by the group through gestures and reactions to them. The members of Motvind and the expert analyst took part as equals in this convening, and the landscapes that became apparent in dialogue became the medium of exchange between personal experiences and expert terminology. Sight is a medium through which the individual may express his or her separate but presumed sharable images, expose them to others' confirmation and recognition, and thereby not only free him or herself from social isolation but also realise his or her ever-latent chance for temporary escape from societal conventions.

As an image in the imagination of any participating subject, a landscape emerges into appearance whenever it becomes the object of an utterance or contemplation. In any such case, landscape emerges as a rebirth, a recollection, an active gathering guided by a concept that provides meaning. The act of imagination itself will blur the distinction between the past and the future, making them appear as modes of the present moment. Any possible appearance is an object of imagination rather than of materiality, whether it is the barn at Orreleiksheia as observed seconds or years ago, or the proposed but not yet constructed towers of the wind turbines. In this sense, the emancipative power of imagination lies in the articulated motif's capacity to connect vision and word in a comprehensible way. According to Arendt, Heidegger was one of the main proponents of such a view, claiming that "*logos* remains tied to vision; if speech separates itself from the evidence given in intuition it degenerates into idle talk which prevents seeing" (Arendt, 1978:118). What this means is that only verbal images, metaphorically performing motifs, will function as nodes of exchange between the conceptual world of the analyst and the experienced world of anyone. We are here returning to the crucial necessity to keep alive the *discrepancy* embedded in the landscape metaphor in order to keep analytically narrated landscapes up to date and capable of conveying relevant insight. We must constantly reinvent or redefine motifs, but in such a way that they still stay true to the enduring mythical pastoral motives that sustain them.

The *action* of the landscape analyst offers an invitation to inhabit an image

The point of departure for any landscape analyst's work is the circumstance that the landscape is always still to be exposed and made apparent. The landscape has not yet emerged into appearance before the analyst has written his or her text, constructed his or her diagrams and created his or her illustrations. Just as the presence of land does not suffice for a landscape to appear to all those present on a site, people's words and documents are not enough for everything to be seen and heard by all those who may be gathered in a place. Whether in a meeting room in Bodø, on a field trip to Vegaøyan or in the dialogue between Tityrus and Meliboeus in Vergil's first *Eclogue*, it is very clear that speech, written words and other utterances only constitute the necessary point of departure for a shared reality to appear. Talking does not affirm reality. Walking the same way or reading the same text does not necessarily lead to the appearance of a shared reality, but it narrows the choice of opportunities decisively. In any case, whether it is a text, a photograph or a strip of land that defines one's sight, whatever the last connection with the material world is, it is from this point that one's *attention* is caught and imagination will be guided.

Since Vergil, the pastoral way of letting landscapes emerge into appearance has been to treat reality imaginatively, but still in relation to contemporary reality. Winsor Leach has described the pastoral narrative as an imaginative scene surrounded by an everyday arena (Leach, 1974:109):

> Although all of these landscapes are imaginary, their careful, deliberate organization makes us understand that they are real to the persons who live within them. To the reader, they should stand as representations of actual scenes. These are the landscapes whose inhabitants are conscious of time and season, aware of living in nature and responsive to its demands. Such landscapes are consistent with a world in which history plays a role: where the real Rome is always in the background and the pastoral setting is only one location within the framework of a greater nature.

As a convening in images, the landscape analysis is initiated by the analyst, and optionally retaken part in by the public. An analytical narrative should always be directed at an engaged subject, as a visual guide. The performance of the analytical narrative should raise landscape awareness in a reader or listener. The analyst should "turn nature into a picture that in turn invites and requires an engaged reader or viewer to bring it to life" (Saunders, 2008:117). Analysing the visual character of a World Heritage Site like Vegaøyan, for example, does not mean pointing to accidental views in the area, or seeing it as an inhabitant of the islands would or through the lenses of local bureaucracies' already existing characterisations of the area. On the contrary, it means remaining loyal to Unesco's narrative and, as J.B. Jackson emphasises, letting anything else "merge into a kind of invisibility" (Jackson, 1984:32) as mere background. It means letting the landscape emerge into appearance through the analytical narrative itself.

The analyst has the privilege of pointing out an area's potential as landscape, but the final commitment to the proposals is always left to the individual reader. As in Vegaøyan, Sarpefossen and Storhei, the visualisations of the landscape analytical utterance offer its readers a point of arrival for their feelings, impressions, sights and thoughts. To accept the invitation of the analytical landscape utterance means to be engaged in the appearance of the landscape on the analyst's terms. In doing so, both the narrator and the listener become equal creators of the shared image (Saunders, 2008:113).

References

Arendt, H. 1978. *The life of the mind*, San Diego, Harcourt.

Arendt, H. 1998. *The human condition*, Chicago, University of Chicago Press.

Bakhtin, M. 2006. *The dialogic imagination: four essays*, Austin, University of Texas Press.

Clark, K. 1961. *Landscape into art*, London, Penguin.

Eagleton, T. 2008. *Literary theory: an introduction – anniversary edition*, Malden, Blackwell.

Fiskevold, M. 2011. *Veien som vilje og forestilling: analysemetoder for landskap og estetisk erfaring*, Ås, Universitetet for miljø- og biovitenskap.

Fiskevold, M. 2016a. *Articulating landscape as common good: common goods from a landscape perspective*, Florence, Uniscape.

Fiskevold, M. 2016b. Vegaøyan verdensarv – visuell karakter: rapport. Oslo, Sweco.

Fiskevold, M. 2016c. *Vision completed: narrating the image of the landscape*, Nagoya, IAIA.

Gadamer, H.-G. 1977. *Die Aktualität des Schönen: Kunst als Spiel, Symbol und Fest*, Stuttgart, Philipp Reclam.

Gadamer, H.-G. 2010. *Sannhet og metode: grunntrekk i en filosofisk hermeneutikk*, Oslo, Bokklubben.

Geelmuyden, A. K. & Fiskevold, M. 2016. Den europeiske landskapskonvensjonen: en pastorale for vår egen tid? *Nordisk Arkitekturforskning*, 28, 51–79.

Jackson, J. B. 1984. *Discovering the vernacular landscape*, New Haven, Yale University Press.

Leach, E. W. 1974. *Vergil's* Eclogues: *landscapes of experience*, Ithaca, Cornell University Press.

Lyotard, J.-F. 1984. *The postmodern condition: a report on knowledge*, Manchester, Manchester University Press.

Potteiger, M. & Purinton, J. 1998. *Landscape narratives: design practices for telling stories*, New York, Wiley.

Ritter, J. 1974. *Subjektivität: sechs Aufsätze*, Frankfurt, Suhrkamp.

Saunders, T. 2008. *Bucolic ecology: Virgil's* Eclogues *and the environmental literary tradition*, London, Duckworth.

Statens Vegvesen. 2014. *V712 Konsekvensanalyser*, Oslo, Vegdirektoratet.

Straus, E. 1956. *Vom Sinn der Sinne: ein Beitrag zur Grundlegung der Psychologie*, Berlin, Springer.

Unesco. 2004. *Vegaøyan: the Vega archipelago – World Heritage Scanned Nominations*, Paris, Unesco.

Unesco world heritage centre. 2008. *Operational guidelines for the implementation of the World Heritage Convention*, Paris, Unesco.

Chapter 5

Articulating analytical narratives of contemporary pastoral landscapes

From human activity to landscapes of reflection

In the previous chapters, we have seen how some essential motives of the pastoral tradition can be traced throughout Western literature, visual art and the design of landscapes. Moreover, landscape motifs from ancient Greek and Roman texts as well as from Renaissance works, where language and sensation, ideals and materiality interact, may still cause landscapes to appear into emergence in the everyday world of today's "shepherds".

Looking again at the shepherds around the tomb in the idyllic setting of the second (Louvre) version of Poussin's painting *Et in Arcadia ego* (Figure 2.3), Panofsky identified "calm discussion" (Panofsky, 1982:313). We may recognise a frozen or suspended action. This divergence in interpretation simultaneously changes the entire motif. Now the motif no longer displays an idea, as Panofsky contends, but the *emergence into appearance* of an idea. When the sight of the dialogue is replaced by the sight of an interrupted communication, it seems more plausible to think that the shepherds' attention is directed to a topic outside the setting. They are gazing more at the spectator than at each other, expecting an answer to a question they apparently do not yet have the capacity to articulate. The existence of death is not yet within the shepherds' horizon. It is as though Poussin has caught the creative act prior to the moment when the landscape emerges into appearance. Like Poussin's shepherds, the narrator of the Telemark account was waiting for an image which was craved but not yet in reach of her perception. She was waiting for a visual guide (an idea of landscape) which could let a motif emerge into appearance before her searching eyes. The utterance was not yet established. What we recognise in the picture, just as in the Telemark account, is the coming into being of a new horizon of comprehension. Accordingly, in the Telemark narrative, the image can be read as a question posed to the readers: how can we speak about landscape in a way that tells us something about our life today and which they can recognise as shared?

In this chapter we shall continue to trace the pastoral motives of *emergence into appearance*, *discrepancy* and *emancipation* and try to answer this question, relating the pastoral motives to activities that affect today's landscape. As the node of our contemporary way of life, we shall look at the road as the primary site for our day-to-day way of experiencing land as landscapes. With both Ritter's genealogy of the modern landscape concept and our choice of contemporary travel as a backdrop together constituting our guiding idea, we shall elaborate pastoral landscapes in three different localities in the vicinity of Oslo. Conceived as verbal utterances in the *polis of the eye*, landscape analytical narratives reflect on the practices of society through the medium of nature. Everyday environments materialise as pastoral motifs and offer a distanced but still passionate view of contemporary human engagement with land. J.B. Jackson has described such motifs in the following way (Jackson, 1994:160):

> So one way of defining such localities would be to say that they are cherished because they are embedded in the everyday world around us and easily accessible, but at the same time are distinct from the world. A visit to them is a small but significant event.

Entirely free of conventional thinking and methodological constraints, we will demonstrate how the analyst can propose imaginative landscape drafts similar to Theocritus' *Idylls* by presenting pastoral landscape motifs derived from ordinary practices belonging to the contemporary road. In that they materialise a pastoral idea, all these motifs represent analytical fragments of what could have become analytical pastoral narratives, articulated in the genre of a photographic essay (Graf, 2013). Every motif is selected and articulated in order to express an aspect of a contemporary humanity-nature unity.

Image formation following the articulation of a motif

In Vergil's *Eclogues*, the reader, the author and the fictional figures themselves are all separated in some way from the described scenes. This distance is exactly what the landscape analyst has to address and take advantage of. As an instant outcome of *labour*, a landscape will be limited to a subject's expressed feelings there and then, and will soon vanish if not taken further. As an enduring outcome of *work*, on the other hand, a landscape will be a more or less fixated image according to conventional ways of representing areas. Only as an outcome of *action* can a sensed or culturally inherited landscape be transformed into a political utterance. The analyst then needs to leave behind the support of the organism, sounds, smells and motion, as well as any preconceived way of presenting land, and rely entirely on his or her own ability to capture the event by the sole means of a language that is relevant to the situation. The analyst has to give his or her own analytical narrative a direction and momentum, thus making the landscape utterance into a statement on its own account.

Analysing landscapes necessarily implies creating a permanence and order (*work*) of some sort out of a phenomenon which has much in common with the flux of nature (*labour*). Thus, the landscape analyst has to mediate the tension between order and disorder, fixation and flux, and prepare the landscape for subjective (pastoral) contemplation. This task has to be accomplished, however, without ever separating it from its contemporary context.

A landscape idea steers how the analyst envisages his object of analysis, the landscape. A guiding idea in Vergil's first *Eclogue*, for instance, is Meliboeus' lost, well-tended farmland and Tityrus' wastefulness. The performed landscape, therefore, lies inherent in the idea, which both initiates and sees the performed utterance through to its completion. It encodes presented verbal images according to a value position or convention. The idea works as an invisible model for the coming motif, *but also* as a basis for evaluating the ensuing image and judging the uttered, proposed landscape. Meliboeus' spoken sentences are what mark Tityrus' starting point, as they introduce him to a scene that he may or may not be able to see. As readers, we understand that Tityrus' not-seeing has to do with the fact that he lacks the idea which could have made the uttered landscape emerge into appearance for himself.

The road provides a shared horizon and common way of life

The spoken sentences mark out Tityrus' or any other receiver's potential starting point for perceiving a piece of land as landscape. Through visible motifs, whether articulated in words, photographs, maps or other illustrations, the reader of an analytical narrative should be guided through an imaginative tour starting from a well-known and widespread practice. For decades now, everyday life has involved entering and leaving the car or other motorised vehicle (Featherstone et al., 2005; Urry, 2007) whereby quotidian sites are connected as nodes in the network of civilisation. The car culture has caused large transformations on the land (Egebjerg and Simonsen, 2005; Morrison and Minnis, 2013), establishing an influential base of reference for cultural production (Borden, 2013), political ideologies (Zeller, 2007) and artistic expression (e.g. Friedlander, 2010). The road, with its intrinsic norms and regulations, provides a scope for conventional perception and a frame for daily practices.

The road serves as a reference on the basis of which pastoral episodes such as that between Meliboeus and Tityrus may take place as proposed by the analyst's text. In the same way, the road serves the reader as a known arena of shared experiences. It should enable anyone to form the images proposed by the analyst. The road involves a material *horizon of movement* and an immaterial *horizon of comprehension*, through its familiar physical layout, its known methods of construction, its authoritative regulations, and its traces of professional cultures and competing agendas. Moreover, with its reliance on customary behaviour and repeated use, it is characterised by a high degree of habit. The road offers a precise geographical reference for both material practices and verbal discourses. It allows us here to assign a pastoral landscape motif to various conditions for human engagement with the land. The materialisation of motifs in the utterance of an analytical landscape should make it possible for the actors of the road to engage in it. Thus, the diverse versions of *practices of travel* on roads, ordinary and widespread at the same time, expert-driven or individually performed, globally standardised or vernacular, etc., take on a role as our reference for an analytical exemplification of the emergence into appearance of contemporary pastoral landscapes.

Land into articulated, material *and* organic *landscapes*

As will be evident from the choice of examples, a pastoral motif can easily be identified both within the road corridor itself and in imaginative extensions of ordinary travel routes. Admitting that the road represents a programming of ways to travel, it bears all the characteristics of a parergon, the background to which the motives of *emergence into appearance, discrepancy* and *emancipation* owe their potency. As an element of power, the road controls anything from body movement to the morals of public behaviour. It functions as a pivot on which modern civilisation and society revolves. The appearance of a landscape and its materialisation in motifs relies for its relevance on this version of the road as one of the contemporary pastoral's negative ideals.

When landscape analysts point at the visible configuration of a site through a descriptive text, pick out photographs or produce drawings to illustrate a future situation, they give their perceptions and ideas visible form as motifs. Articulated according to traditional pastoral motives, motifs are results of the landscape analyst's own *action*. They simultaneously visualise a historical, conceptual and visual path, and they indicate a direction for future engagement and activity. The shown motifs, regarded as the analyst's proposals, thereby make a claim as to how real sites should be perceived visually. As long as this claim is motivated by the will to bring a new way of seeing into the world, making something *emerge into appearance*, disclosing a current *discrepancy* and revealing a potential for *emancipation*, the practice of analysing landscapes has a legitimate mission to complete.

A motif does not reconstruct a landscape, but visually proposes a certain humanity-nature relation in an area. It is a materialised *reflection* of different ways in which humans receive and engage with a problematic nature. As an instance of the landscape analyst's own *action*, the motifs of the analyst are laid out as stepping stones for the reader's memory, activating the necessary *labour, work* and *action* in order to be conceived as intended. As the articulated landscape of Edelgranveien, the material landscape of Vækerø and the organic landscape of Kustein will show, these landscapes are created primarily with the support of imaginative *action, work* and *labour*, realised by the participants of the *polis of the eye*. Any transaction of land into landscape is shared through a fundamental activity which frames the land in a defined way.

Edelgranveien as articulated landscape

Articulating a response to habitual road experiences in Edelgranveien

In one of Oslo's suburbs, a road called Edelgranveien leads into an ordinary housing area. It looks like any other suburban road: the pavement is separated from the tarmac-covered roadway; there are street lights at regular intervals, and guard rails prevent vehicles from rolling off the road at critical spots. As an engineered construction, Edelgranveien meets the local transport requirements. Body and vehicle are offered the same materiality and the same layout. Their respective material imprints on the surface differ in scale, but share fundamental design. As a whole, a road (path, street etc.) appears as a standardised corridor whose prime aim is to ensure the smoothness of everyday circulation.

If we accept these premises, the identification of pastoral landscape motifs in the area becomes a matter of comprehension more than of site experience. It raises the question of how an everyday scene can be transformed into visual motifs of the *landscape concept*. With the articulation of a motif, the analyst gives the landscape concept a specific form. An *action* is effectuated when the pastoral landscape as *way of seeing* is practised in an everyday road environment. Although surrounded by the normalising road corridor, we have the option to mentally stray away from the ordinary instrumentality of travelling and instead begin searching for pastoral landscape motifs along the road. Potential motifs emerge into appearance as outstanding, vital contrasts to the ordinariness of the road.

Emergence into appearance: visualising a modern pastoral

When we walk on Edelgranveien, equipped with the pastoral landscape idea, we might be able to recognise landscapes in natural materials such as stones and trees, in natural processes such as rain and daylight, or in the human adaptation to or fragmentation of the natural surface. As an imaginative response to an ideal unity between humanity and nature, the pastoral landscape ideal itself materialises by means of the land, as the land is framed and articulated within the scope of the idea. Nowhere is this relation between humanity and nature more apparent than in the ephemeral changes of light, for example in the motif of the illuminated darkness

Figure 5.1 Wet snowfall on Edelgranveien.

of night (Figure 5.1). On Edelgranveien, artificial lighting casts light and shadows at a land cut which is the result of the road's construction through a ridge. The steep slopes of the cut rise where the illuminated field ends. At the end of winter, when the temperature rises and an occasional heavy and wet snowfall fills the air, the natural cycle of water becomes apparent as rays of light against a black sky; as increasing amounts of wet snow gradually cover the barren rocks, even though they are not lit, they start shimmering, and the adjacent ground gradually takes on lighter and lighter greys, letting emerge into appearance the entire backdrop of the illuminated corridor, almost imperceptibly. Evening snowfall in Edelgranveien shows the road as fixed stage for the exchange of verbal images.

For the inhabitants of the nearby homes and within the horizon of a routine commute, if it is noticed at all, Edelgranveien represents a habitual time lapse, hardly a landscape. However, a landscape image may emerge in parallel to ordinary perception, as a sort of suspension of it. Each single event of landscape perception is the *ideal expression* of a reflective mindset, of its character and relevance (the character of *action*). The overall image that is retained and given general validity as *characteristic* of the area arises out of a reflective act and mirrors the acting subject's ability to recognise and hold onto nature's presence. This is why the cliffs and eroding stones of the land cut in the previous motif are seen as indicators of the cycle of nature and not of danger and potential accidents. The scene and its major features

Figure 5.2 Roadside weeds.

lend their materiality to a landscape concept. This is also why another scene appears as a pastoral landscape motif when inscribed into modernity's pastoral idea. A footpath framed by flowering weeds, its surface still covered with the grit of winter maintenance, shows natural wilderness and human adaptation to it in the same image (Figure 5.2). The motif is pastoral because it is a result of and activates a critical creativity within the frame of programmed existence. The pastoral motif shows itself in the attention to seasonal change, or as a willing acceptance and adaptation to all naturally given site conditions.

A pastoral landscape motif emerges into appearance even more clearly when it is perceived in an everyday and ordinary environment. Even after a heavy snowfall, there is nothing extraordinary about Edelgranveien. Its layout and measurements are exactly like those of any other similar road. It is a product of construction manuals and conventions. Equally, the ordinary design of the road makes it representative of a situation which is shared by most travellers. Edelgranveien represents a well-known and predictable scene. It is as expected. It thus represents a stable backdrop which contrasts different events as they may emerge into appearance. These landscape events may take place at any time and at any spot along the road. For example, in passing a junction this morning, after the snowfall, we may notice how one part of the road is cleared while the other is still decidedly covered with snow. We notice how the obstructing snow is more tolerated in one of the

Figure 5.3 Slush at a road crossing.

streets, the street which currently is not cleaned, than on Edelgranveien. It might seem trivial, but this little comparison makes the pastoral landscape emerge into appearance as a product of language's capacity to create motifs at sites where nature's still free forces are noticed within an otherwise controlled environment. The natural cycles appear as such in relation to the expectation of the road as a slick belt of black tarmac. Visually, both convention and exception are emphasised in the same motif. As a product of *action*, the pastoral landscape motif is activated when purposeful reflection guides the image formation and its articulation.

Discrepancy: visualising the dynamics of the landscape concept through creative recollection

Without a modern pastoral landscape idea, the weeds on the verge and the grit covering the tarmac would have remained isolated elements: weeds and grit. It is the idea of humanity's unity with nature that makes these features of the land into a visible landscape motif. Once visualised as a pastoral motif, the relations between these signs of regulated versus free nature are set into play. The flowering weeds are cut once or twice every summer, while in between, the slope slowly resumes its natural state. The grit remnants bear witness to the past winter and the necessary protection against slippery ice on the path. Space becomes a scene where several episodes in time are evoked simultaneously, as in a *chronotope* (Bakhtin, 2006). It is as though the sight of the wild weeds and the grit respectively set in motion an imaginative process that in an instant fulfils the cycle of nature, which otherwise takes place over time. The landscape pastoral is an example of humanity's capacity to posit itself temporarily alongside if not outside of everyday life, in a culturally enriching way. The emotional confrontations with reality furnish memory with options. Keeping these impressions alive, any scene once experienced can be compared with the scene which momentarily dominates our sight. Remembrance and imagination transform the motif of weeds and grit on Edelgranveien into symbolic components of the concept itself.

The visual appearance of the cyclical changes in nature can be apprehended just under the soles of our shoes. Grit covers the pavement. The melting snow becomes water flowing on the surface. At night, the process stops, the wet tarmac gradually dries up, emerging as a uniformly grey, pebbled surface with a dead string of dirty snow along its edge. In the daytime, the melting process resumes. Both natural forces and human actions make the cyclical changes visible. In these images (Figure 5.4) they occur as episodes, revealing to the attentive eye an array of previous events as well as events that will take place in the future. The snow will fall again; it will be swept away from the road surface and left in the ditch that has been planned for this kind of temporary storage. The snow masses assembled by human labour will expand and shrink and eventually disappear totally, returning as water into the cyclical processes of nature. As the image shows, both natural

Figure 5.4 Melting snow.

and human forces act in accordance with and thus as indicators of the cycles of nature.

Just like the tomb in Arcadia, the negative ideal inherent in pastoral representation is always in sight of anyone engaged in analysing landscapes. Just as the melting snow visualises the ephemeral presence of each season, so does the black tarmac under the cover of loose grit and filth when it is cleaned once a year. The negative ideal of the modern pastoral landscape may emerge into appearance in the surface of the sweating bitumen (Figure 5.5). Primarily, the black tarmac appears as a sign of the public provision of safe and reliable transport arteries. However, even the road may become the materialisation and visible sign of discursive conflicts in society as different human interests want the road to function in certain, often incommensurable ways. The public roads administration wants it to be an efficient carriageway without risk of fatal accidents. The adjacent local communities want it to be a safe and noise-free transport artery. Business enterprises want it to be an efficient and predictable link in a production and distribution chain. And the tourist industry wants it to be an easy access to attractions. Every interest is a carrier of meaning, derived from and applied to the road.

From melting snow to black tarmac, from the diversity of ephemeral natural occurrences to the diversity of societal regulations, the discrepancies of the positive and negative ideals and their appearances in the land as well as in societal discourses lay the foundation for a rich and enlightening imagery concerning the contemporary world. All observations along a journey on a

Figure 5.5 Black tarmac.

road, from the never-ending and never-beginning of nature's processes to the everlasting calculating efforts of modern society (*work*), thus obtain both tangible presence and narrative relevance from their pastoral motivation. If we trace the associations (Latour, 2005) attached to both melting snow and black tarmac back to their imaginative point of intersection, a new reality appears as present in the world of the storyteller: "Action reveals itself fully only to the storyteller, that is, to the backward glance of the historian, who indeed always knows better what it was all about than the participants" (Arendt, 1998:192). In accordance with Arendt, analysed landscapes investigate the horizon of a motif, searching in the archives of positive and negative ideals for its changing applicability. As an outcome of this exploration, the practice of analysing landscapes is an action that always implies a new approach to the contemporary landscape. The motivating discrepancy in the pastoral response to land means that every analytical narrative implies an explicit exploration of ways to conceptualise land as landscape. Just as we saw in the narrative of the gunshot, the plot of the pastoral narrative implies that the discrepancies between negative and positive are never meant to be solved but continuously renewed.

Emancipation: visualising the recurrence of the concept

A road like Edelgranveien could be conceived as a route of transportation, an object of maintenance or the site for an inventory of elements. The road could even be regarded as a landscape with no outstanding or inherent values. In any case, these observations are all conventional ways of seeing the area, and they are all influencing norms, articulated and properly described in manuals or expressed in common opinions. But, as Arendt stresses, action and speech are ways to let new beginnings enter into the play of the world (Arendt, 1998:204). One morning we may observe a concentration of footprints along the inside of the ridge formed by cleared snow (Figure 5.6). Another evening we observe the tracks of a lonely skier departing or arriving from the nearby woods. But what we may recognise in these traces is creativity and adaptation to the current state of the road: it is less the movement of a traveller than his or her conceptual departure from the conventional way of seeing and his or her observant approach to the land in its current state. The restorative powers of the pastoral landscape are not so much a property inherent in the land; on the contrary, subjective restoration depends more on the individual's capacities to see, remember and imagine, and to find in his or her own subjective imagination the relevant solution in relation to the potential of the site.

The traces of both footprints and ski tracks are fragments of such subjective engagement with land. The appearance and discrepancy of the motif lay the foundation for individuals to evaluate, make decisions and choose their own way of engaging with the land. Departing from the cleared and smooth

Figure 5.6 Ski tracks on the roadside.

corridor which allows movement in a lot of different directions, the entering of the still uncleared path requires a certain capacity to choose, and implies an awareness of the state of the land: where should we proceed with our journey? We have to cross the line of the snowbank at an appropriate point and proceed along a path which it is up to us to define (Figure 5.7). Modernity's pastoral idea is thereby visualised in the motif of the track on the snowbank. The motif shows the material consequences of a choice, but it does not show whether this choice has had any emancipating effect on the landscaping individual. This interpretation is the analyst's own contribution, and it is an outcome of the analyst giving pastoral motives visual shape in the chosen motifs of an analytical narrative. The image proposed in the analytical narrative offers an aesthetically sustainable insight, because it shows how any area can give the subject an opportunity to look beyond conventional or routine perception. It thus affords the resourceful individual a space on the margins of societal regulations and expectations (society's programme). It is the kind of visualisation which cannot be captured within a prescribed procedure or methodological model. The lack of institutionalisation is compensated for by the articulation of a guiding idea. Renouncing conventional ways of seeing and expressing a landscape opens up an entirely new opportunity for paying attention to and elaborating motifs according to a pastoral attitude.

The welfare state's claim to take care of everyone's interests, as if it were an extension of the private realm, leaves few spaces for the independent

Figure 5.7 Crossing the snowbank.

virtues of the individual. The subject's talent for experiencing life not only
as one of an uncountable group but also as a unique version of earthly existence only has secondary status in modern society. This is what led Ritter
to claim that *landscape* supplies the modern subject with an opportunity
to get involved in his or her environment through his or her own aesthetic
engagement.

To engage in a world means a potential emancipation both from the natural
bonds of the *animal laborans* and from the social conformity of the *homo
faber*. The road, infused as it is with all sorts of societal arrangements, offers
a scene where human contemplation is stimulated by the urge to add something more, see something different from what is officially set before it: on the
edge of the land cut, for instance, some children have built a small wooden
hut out of branches and boards. This close to Edelgranveien, this is one of
the area's few traces of real, aesthetic engagement with land. The pastoral
landscape motif of the hut displays the pastoral motivation of emancipation,
which arises from partaking in and realising the potential of a piece of land
that is otherwise only characterisable as a "space left over after planning".

The creative re-cognition of the richness of the human world means that
an analyst has to take care of the historical resilience of the pastoral landscape idea without turning it into something literal, as a location, a name, a
picture or a physical setting. This is what has happened, for example, in the
case of Dælivannet, where the symbolism of the painting may lose power in

confrontation with the picture's reproduction on site. The second challenge of the analyst is to maintain the essence of pastoral motivation and translate its motives into contemporary motifs. Both challenges are met, in the first case as reinterpretations of culturally inherited images, in the second case as contemporary products of aesthetic sensibility. They are both required of the analyst to create visual proposals, to which other participants in the *polis of the eye* can respond.

The material landscape of Vækerø

Confronting persistent human intentionality as it can be ascribed to the area around the Vækerø estate

The estate of Vækerø is situated on the outskirts of the city of Oslo. Today, it is delimited by a motorway (E18) to the south-west, and by the Oslo fjord on the opposite side. Parts of a park around the original old buildings are preserved, even though several large office buildings have been constructed within the green space. A broad, paved plaza serves as entrance area to the new office complex and connects a junction on the motorway to the natural coastline. The whole area is well designed, maintained and under constant surveillance. The access from the motorway to some large underground car parks is arranged as a traffic system with high capacity. Minor elements such as fences block possible shortcuts for pedestrians in order to ensure safety for all travellers. The whole estate bears the signs of a thoroughly planned environment, that is, of being the materialisation of a *model*, where every element is assigned a premeditated role.

Transport models, road manuals and computer programs are all objectified intentions, which in turn are inscribed onto the surface of the earth as infrastructure areas. The pastoral landscape motif is also a part of this material scene, but draws its legitimacy from a horizon beyond the roadside slopes, prescribed lane widths or painted guidelines on the tarmac. On Edelgranveien, we identified the pastoral landscape motif as an outcome of responses to land use discourses. At Vækerø, the decisive component of a material landscape motif lies neither in a rhetorical approach nor in an organic experience, but in the layout of the surface of the land itself. Acting as *work*, the landscape pastoral motif is created when we let the layout of the grounds itself guide the image formation. The motif mediates the features which are articulated as the character of the surface.

Appearance: visualising pastoral motifs departing from the character of the terrain

Arendt describes the human fabrication of things as an endeavour which brings nature to a standstill. Fundamental changes to the surface of the earth represent complex versions of such things. The land is modified and arranged in a way which suits human needs and as they are conceived in an idea, an imagined model (Arendt, 1998:140):

> The actual work of fabrication is performed under the guidance of a model in accordance with which the object is constructed. This model can be an image beheld by the eye of the mind or a blueprint in which the image has already found a tentative materialization through work. In either case, what guides the work of fabrication is outside the fabricator and precedes this actual work process.

In a human-made environment of *work*, the pastoral landscape motif owes its presence to the emergence into appearance of the terrain's natural or human-made character. The idealising aspects of the idea of landscape are no longer merely articulated and illustrated in words, but actually located or even inscribed into the land's surface. The steps leading from the coastal promenade at Vækerø down to the pebbled beach are material outcomes of such a model and guided by an idea (Figure 5.8). The granite steps offer a convenient way to the shore. Conceived as a pastoral landscape motif, they simultaneously display the abrupt transition between land and sea, especially at spring tides. Emphasised by the slight elevation provided by each step, the steps furthermore show the variations in land form, from the coastline and as it continues inland. At the same time, we know that the layout of the site and the arrangement of the steps are pre-shaped in advanced computer software. The constructor has carried out the instructions of the software and thereby has materialised the ideas of the programmer.

Through *work*, the human world fabricates, opposes and changes the natural cycle and surface of a site according to a certain idea or intention. On the estate of Vækerø, the process of altering the surface of the ground has been practised continually for several hundred years, rapidly accelerating in recent times. The current outcome of this process is an area whose materiality has changed fundamentally since the time when it was only a part of the Oslo fjord's shore. Vækerø was originally a place where timber from the nearby forests was stored before being exported to central Europe. The farmhouse was transformed into a manor in 1880. At the same time, a large park was laid out surrounding the house. The nearby road between the cities of Oslo and Drammen, Drammensveien, was equally enlarged and has since continued to grow. In the 1950s, it was moved away from the manor's entrance gate, and a new junction was constructed, followed by the office complex of Norsk Hydro in 1985, parallel to the little ridge delimiting the estate to the south. The junction was again enlarged. The last step so far in the alterations of the Vækerø grounds is a new building complex from 2008, including a plaza which serves as an entrance area to all the buildings, a meeting place for the employees as well as a passage for

Figure 5.8 Steps down to the shore at Vækerø.

pedestrians to and from the beach. The west façade of the newest complex and the open space of the plaza mirror the orientation of the buildings from the 1980s (Figure 5.9). The plaza also enhances the view and the possibility to move from the strictly regulated realm of the big road down towards the seaside and the wide horizon of the fjord. What this brief history of the groundworks shows is that the successive alterations neither constitute mere transformations of nature into a human-made environment nor appear as a total replacement of the place's a natural character. On the contrary, the appearance of the material landscape shows how adding and removing earth and elements can eventually create an image of the land that is mainly constituted by its physical arrangement.

All these material alterations, intentionally modelled and successively carried out, each time leaving the area in a new state, are still but a part of a landscape pastoral motif, and can still be shown to characterise the place in a unique way. Additionally, the view of the plaza towards the fjord and the view from the shore embracing a vast seascape are also decisive parts of the motif. The visibility of this pastoral landscape motif requires that it is narratively localised in a larger area than that which is actually modified. The changes are part of an overall composition, the place's design. Thus, the idea of the Vækerø landscape encompasses areas that visually are borrowed from further out, forming part of a planned scenery. Approaching the shore, the motif is developed between the limits of our sight and the tangible limits of

Figure 5.9 Entrance plaza at Vækerø.

our body's reach. Our eyes might catch sight of the far horizon around the fjord between the trunks of the birches and firs. Every tree, every wall and piece of ground is arranged in a manner that alternately hides and reveals the borderline between sky and earth. We cannot see through the terrace's massive blocks of stone, but have to follow the wall right to the edge where the regularly cut stones end and the eternity of the sky begins. At this point, previously hidden by a bend of the landform, the coastal promenade becomes visible (Figure 5.10). It stands as a wall juxtaposed to the bay. Nevertheless, this materialised design attitude does not display an intention to conquer or besiege nature. The path mirrors the meandering of the shore. The waves are allowed to meet the construction, albeit not on natural but on human conditions. With the far horizon in sight and the busy motorway as a fading image behind us, the walk along the shore connects imageries of past and present. What we see is composed from layers of alterations, each representing natural forces and human intentions imprinted on the surface of the earth.

Discrepancy: visualising the permanence of the land surface

Human-made changes to the surface, small or fundamental, are almost always carried out intentionally and as a part of some overall idea. Every levelling of the ground, every direction of motion, indeed our entire movement

Figure 5.10 Promenade along the shore at Vækerø.

through this land is prepared and foreseen by generations of planners and architects. However unable they have been to direct individual thoughts and attention, the arrangement of the ground and the inscription of previous influential decision makers' intentions are still present to us. Here, the landscape image is of a *designed arrangement* of material elements from different historical phases, each having left traces that emphasise different aspects of the site. Moving through the area, one can observe various objects which all, each in their own way, are part of divergent horizons of comprehension. The area can be perceived as a landscape with durability and continuity. The strip of land between the fjord and the office complex adjacent to the motorway must be understood as a material arrangement which prepares our step and directs our vision. All these appearances are products of human *work*, as embedded in the material layout of the ground, and they appear as a part of a shared, human world. As Arendt concludes, "[w]ithout a world between men and nature, there is eternal nature, but no objectivity" (Arendt, 1998:137). When we place our foot on the gritted and levelled ground, we hardly need to examine it any further; in fact, our doing so was foreseen years ago. Entering this piece of land, we are simultaneously entering a landscape of inherited imagination. The pathway running along the shore, the terrace in front of the manor house, the beach trees and the fields, they are all material remnants of older motifs, but still represent options for seeing this land as a landscape today. As Arendt observes, the *work* of the human world gives images permanence, even though the area's materiality has fundamentally changed over the last hundred years. However, the inherited motifs are simultaneously motifs which conceal a discrepancy in human motivations. The fabrication of the surface can be recognised as revealing both the positive pastoral ideal that reinforces the durable character of the surface and the negative ideal that has formed the surface according to past times' standards of utility and efficiency.

The additions to the ground have been made gradually, on every occasion borrowing or replacing a further part of the naturally shaped land. As we ramble the shoreline along the constructed pathway, our sight moves back and forth from the openness of the sea to the shadows of the trees and bushes, from the undulating horizon to the firm ground, and from the eternity of the sky to the immediate proximity of walls, steps and rails. The elements located along the path make us well aware of the character of the site. But they seem like small preparations compared with the effects of the newly constructed boardwalk passing the outcrop at the southern edge of the estate (Figure 5.11). The combination of the wooden floor and the bend in the handrail emphasises the character of the land form. Moreover, the construction has made it possible to avoid big alterations to the little cliff and gives the rambler a revelatory view over the entire seascape. Also, the easy walk transmits the perspective of our vision from body to mind. We are invited to receive these images, as are other ramblers that we meet

Figure 5.11 Boardwalk passing a steep cliff.

on our way, and as have visitors of bygone and future eras. The line of sight weaves together thoughts of past and present. The arrangement of objects and the guiding path give the succession of views a comprehensible order. The recognisable elements form a place to leave, remember and visit again. We realise that we might recollect these well-known images at a later time. The optional re-experience of images, notably in another version, the experience of differing sameness, the recognition of the path, ensures the durability of the place as landscape.

Leaving one of the numerous bus lines at the stop on the motorway at Vækerø, visitors to the area are channelled into one of two possible pedestrian ways to the entrance plaza. They are both exactly three metres wide, fenced by walls and rails, and constantly maintained in order to ensure a safe and dust-free walk from the stop to the indoor facilities of the office buildings. Both ways, constructed according to the manuals of their time, lead through a narrow tunnel which facilitates direct access to the plaza beneath one of the many access ramps of the motorway junction (Figure 5.12). The tunnel width allows for encounters with pedestrians as well as for small tractors and other maintenance vehicles. The ground, the walls and the roof are all made of concrete. The passage through the tunnel is preconceived according to a model whose guiding idea is efficient motion between nodes in a coordinate system. Materialising a model of transport, the tunnel represents the counterforce to the positive pastoral ideal at Vækerø because

Figure 5.12 Pedestrian tunnel.

it reduces and standardises the field of possible pastoral action. Any software implies decisions. These decisions are not made by the perceiver, but their consequences are carried out by the users of the road. The models are programmed by engineers, operated by the planner and lastly executed by the user. In this respect, they are all united by the functionality and lastly the permanence of the intention behind computer software.

The tunnel and the boardwalk, situated at opposite ends of the Vækerø grounds, each represent mutually opposing human attitudes to how the road as human artefact should become part of the surface of the earth. The boardwalk shows careful treatment of the natural terrain, leaving a motif of landscape awareness and composition: half nature and half human rearrangement. The tunnel, on the other hand, arranges the terrain as the result of a calculation of sheer practicality. Even if it displays a landscape of continuous shifts between programmed route and free scenery, any discrepancy in a landscape motif resides more in the narrator's *attitude* towards the character of the site as displayed in his or her analytical description of it, e.g. of the boardwalk and tunnel, than in the diversity of lasting arrangements on the ground. Crossing along the boardwalk, we can participate in the ever-changing displays of nature as they may emerge at exactly this place. Opposite to that, passing comfortably through the tunnel, whether in summer or winter, we could be anywhere in the world. The treatment of the natural surface as it is negotiated through the boardwalk therefore represents a different version of permanence from the durability which is inherent in the underground passage. Only the former shows a pastoral attitude. In both cases, the levelling of the ground has put a definite end to the natural character of the terrain. Sustaining a rest of natural character within human artefacts, however, leaves to the imagination a trace of the original ground, with which any human addition may be compared and in relation to which it may be seen. This imaginative potential owes its enduring force to both the natural character of the site and the human engagement with exactly that aspect, and not least to the dialectic interplay of these which a human contribution may bring to life.

Emancipation: visualising the integrity of the land surface

The epitomic events of movement displayed in the motifs of the boardwalk and tunnel at Vækerø – the layout of the former referring to the natural character of the ground, and that of the latter to the software of public transport – are both the result of models and planning devices. However, when they are treated as pastoral landscape motifs, only the boardwalk enables the subject to recognise its own participation in a continuation of the earth's natural state. The tunnel, on the contrary, exemplifies a common, constructed element belonging to the ever-increasing realm of a virtual reality. It is virtual because merely instrumental, and moreover to humans alone. In our longing for predictability and stability, we tend to see the *works* of this attitude as equivalent to any other material reality. We happily endow the bits and bytes of programmers with the same legitimacy as land that is physically shaped by nature or humanity. Vision is reduced to acceptance of the calculated models displayed on monitors. But as Arendt stresses, the powerful and suggestive motivation of convention is just another means to support thoughtlessness (Arendt, 1978:4):

> Clichés, stock phrases, adherence to conventional, standardized codes of expression and conduct have the socially recognized function of protecting us against reality, that is, against the claim on our thinking attention that all events and facts make by virtue of their existence.

The road, an integrated part of the societal ideal of predictability and efficiency, is similarly infused with codes of conduct and expected behaviour. We are not allowed to cross the motorway, and there are physical objects such as fences and rails which block every attempt to walk directly to the entrance gate of the buildings at Vækerø (Figure 5.13). In this way, the road as a material element works as a component in the software of movement regulation. But the end product of the model equally results in entropy for the pastoral landscape. The durability of the natural surface is replaced by the limited life span of the program. The emancipating powers of pastoral

Figure 5.13 Motorway corridor.

Figure 5.14 Reefs.

motivation stress the fact that there is a choice of action inherent in the natural surface of the ground. On the estate of Vækerø, we will be able to identify different versions of human *work* and how they are inscribed into the surface of land. Walking between the motorway and the shore, we see that the landscape of the site is upheld both by the ephemeral presence of snow on the cliffs, soon to be swept away by the tide (Figure 5.14), and by the regular stream of traffic that is never to come to an end. If permanence is all that is demanded from a material *landscape*, any state of the surface will do. Both the solids of the reefs and the levelled surface of the motorway will stay unaltered and last for future generations. But, unlike the standardised lanes of the road, the location of the reefs lets us distinguish this landscape from other landscapes. Planning landscapes implies a choice. If a pier is constructed on the shore, the presence of the reefs may be gone for ever. The materialisation of one element excludes the presence of another. One construction may deny the alternatives their existence. If the entropy of perceptive diversity resulting from the dominance of materialised virtual reality is to be checked, there is an urgent need to keep the natural character of the surface recognisable.

Withdrawing from the levelled ground of the terrace in front of the manor of Vækerø, we see a succession of landscapes which all accentuate the natural character of the land (Figure 5.15). As we view the fjord, a pastoral landscape motif emerges into appearance. It is framed by the distant but

Figure 5.15 Terrace between Vækerø manor house and the seashore.

still close motorway, its distant time of construction and the distant horizon across the water. The view thereby presents a contemporary experiential node which fuels the imagination with images of mobility, efficiency, cultural heritage and natural land forms. The view from the terrace at Vækerø offers a succession of landscapes beyond the limitations of everyday life. There is just a few minutes' stroll between the sites of these different motifs. Literally around the corner of the motorway, we find ourselves in the middle of a modern business park or among the remnants of an old manor. Metaphorically, this bend in the road simultaneously means the continuation of earlier events. Any standstill means a rebirth of images, every change in the material conservation of the area represents a threat to their continued emergence. As a component of subjective identity, landscape is dependent on the objectivity of material permanence in order to be shared by humankind and people. As Arendt states, people "can retrieve their sameness, that is, their identity, by being related to the same chair and the same table" (Arendt, 1998:137). The durability of an image is in need of an external reference in order to be perceived by a group at the same time and by an individual at different times. As we approach the stone terrace in front of the manor, the walls stand as references to distant times and spaces. Visually sweeping the surface of the granite blocks, our gaze is occupied in time as well in space. We are replicating sceneries that were imagined by generations before us, and we lose our sight in the narrow opening in the horizon framed by the two distant hills. Although we cannot observe their movement, we know that the hills have risen since the last ice age, and we know that they still are continuing their ascent towards the sky. Beyond visibility, we know that the trees and shrubs that cover the surface are of the same age as the ground, and we know that they will continue to grow when even our grandchildren have greeted them for the last time. As we remember the system of the motorway, the *Et in Arcadia ego* of today, it is as though the material contrast provokes the imagery of historical depth, bringing to life ages of events that come into being imaginatively in the same viewshed.

Since the manor was built and the park laid out, the content of the motif itself has changed, although the area is still emblematic of a pastoral legacy. The landscape pastoral image is sustained although society has gone through remarkable transformations. Urban civilisation has crept beyond the original city centre of Kristiania (Oslo) and now surrounds the place. Meadows have been replaced by modern infrastructure, the timber harbour has been replaced by leisure boats, and the houses used for timber storage have today given way to a vast construction-material warehouse. But the area around the manor is kept in or close to its original state. The apparent disconnectedness of the 1880s main building from today's motorway entails a shift in horizon, and the attractiveness of the park stands out in contrast to the road's noisy and steered experience. On the opposite side of the house, looking out from the parterre, the 145-year-old vista over the Oslo fjord gives the visitor the opportunity to share a horizon that is free (and can set one free) from prevalent contemporary practices and values. The presented motif offers an aesthetically sustainable insight, because it reveals how the built environment may be an opportunity for human beings to see themselves and their existence in relation to society's overall order and latent state of change. The area offers scenes which sustain generations through their sensuous presence and by drawing attention to their historical existence. A single tree, as part of a scene, stands as a witness to the prevalence of this temporal and as such indifferent world. Moreover, in the artistry of the melting snow or rain across every threshold from one carved stone to another, the design of the area produces an image that reflects how time leaves traces in an area (Figure 5.16). The motif thus invites the visitor to see connections and to place him- or herself within the ongoing human transformation of the material environment. The motif is pastoral because it activates a person's awareness of his or her encounter with tradition, which she or he otherwise only takes conscious part in sporadically and in a distant way. Terrestrial identity, the continuation of the surface of earth in each person's subjective biography, shows how humanity takes a firm stand against the flow of nature on this liminal strip of land and at this short instance of human existence. Terrestrial identity means an active and binding obligation to engage in the possibilities offered by seeing land as landscape. The shared inheritance, stored in the surface of the land, offers

Figure 5.16 Sculpted water channel.

the opportunity for a revelatory act of seeing which relates the self of each individual to the current material state of the earth.

The organic landscape of Kustein

Experiencing bodily reactions as part of the natural organism of Kustein

Some kilometres into the forested hills surrounding the centre of Oslo, we find the little tarn of Kusteinstjern, one of the sources of the river Lysakerelva, which flows into the Oslo fjord in the suburban township and transport hub of Lysaker. The transport systems which are fully integrated into the urban fabric of places like Lysaker eliminate physical friction on the ground and simultaneously optimise the consumption performed through mobility. In this particular mode of travel, enclosed within a steel case and screened off from the impact of outdoor variations, a mere stay in the open air appears as an existence on the fringes of urbanity. The transition from the standardised road onto the trails in a barren wilderness is yet another way to enter the pastoral landscape. The act of moving between the car's interior and open space creates a plurality of perspectives which is not fully noticed and explored in landscape planning and analysis. The area around the little tarn of Kusteinstjern is part of a nature reserve, protected by law for its pristine forest and wildlife. Access to the area is restricted to cross-country skiing in winter and walking in summer. The absence of roads and motorised traffic offers the rambler a temporary and very different horizon of movement compared with everyday urban landscapes. Images of the area as landscape are shaped as an integrated part of moving. As *labour*, a pastoral landscape motif becomes visible when body and ground assist the eye in the perception of the land as landscape. The body *and* the materiality it negotiates, usually via a modulating vehicle (shoes or skis in this case), represent a unit, an *organism*. The perception of the environment as a sensuous, natural entity is sustained in that the subject is part of the organism. The organic landscape of Kustein is a landscape which evolves as the subject makes its way across the land, effectuating the rhythm of the ground.

Appearance: visualising the accidental presence of the organism

Arendt stresses that the outcome of *labour* is that life is sustained. She is primarily thinking of the bodily consumption and production of food and energy. However, when transposed into the context of human engagement with land as landscape, the notion of *labour* could also include the human body extended as incorporated into the body of the earth. The labour of motion is perceived by the performing subject as an organic reaction to the land. Simultaneously, in visual terms, moving through the woods is a continuous appearance and disappearance of the immediate ground. Seeking a way through the dense forest, we realise that the possible viewpoints and angles are numerous. The features of the land resemble a scene which, as a unity, can never be perceived from one single point of view. The continuing irregularities which we are feeling under our feet at the same time take on visible shapes in front of our eyes, almost mirroring the irregular ground, but not exactly. The dark trunks stand as organic columns in front of the light foliage (Figure 5.17). Some leave space to pass, others do not. Along with our movements, we gradually experience the depth in the picture, which otherwise would have seemed like a flat surface. The elevations and transitions that continuously expose and hide scenes of the area cannot exist without our bodily movement through the land. The eyes serve as recorders of colours and greyscales, while the body incessantly perceives the resistance of the ground.

Vision alone would never have brought us within reach of understanding the trees as clues to where to pass and which places to avoid. The appearance of the area is a result of the labour and presence of our body. And while we are moving, the visible horizon changes in relation to our current standpoint and view. Erwin Straus has emphasised this ephemeral character of visions by comparing the experienced landscape to the geographical model of it, the *work* of the map (Straus, 1956:335, our translation):

Figure 5.17 Rambler's view of the trunks and foliage.

In a landscape, we are enclosed by a horizon; as we wander, the horizon steadily wanders with us. Geographical space has no horizons. When we attempt to orientate ourselves somewhere, ask somebody else about the right way or even pull out a map, we fix/determine our here as a location in a space without horizon.

The ever-shifting horizon, the transitory line between land, water and sky almost concealed within the solids of the forest, is entirely revealed as we reach the summit of the little peak of Kustein. The alternate appearance and disappearance of the horizon is most clearly exposed in the transition between forest and moors that open like narrow pockets in the higher parts of the land. Its visual diversity evolves continuously, in rhythm with our movement.

In addition to the clues offered by vision, experiences of the land are fundamentally dependent on the ground being accessible at all. As we move through an area like that around Kustein, it becomes apparent that any previously experienced route might change with the seasons. As water freezes to ice, the land expands into one solid surface covering the whole area. Contrariwise, when the ice melts, lakes and moors again perforate the surface and render pieces of land inaccessible for the moving body (Figure 5.18). The track crossing the tarn is replaced by a route which surrounds the tarn.

Figure 5.18 Melting tarn.

However, easy access does not only change according to the seasons. Transformations can happen far more rapidly. Pausing for some minutes on our way, we may watch the continuously shifting appearance of the edge between the ski track and the snow-covered moor (Figure 5.19). We can watch the wind carrying drifts of snow over the little ridge, constantly depositing some of it in the track. We can watch the resulting fluctuation of shadows and how they mirror the shifting drifts, and at the same time how they vary from dark white to light black, depending on the ever-shifting presence of clouds and sun.

Discrepancy: visualising the cycles of the organism

As noted above, the changes in the horizon are accompanied by the undulations of the ground. The subject, participating in the unit of the organism with his or her body, experiences the route as an outcome of travelling itself. It is the rhythm afforded by movement, in which the body and ground are gathered by means of some vehicle, which makes for the distinctness of the ground. Together, they make for an emotionally perceived route where the diversity of sights merges with the *labour* of movement. Thus, movement through the land parallels one of the basic principles of the labouring activity itself: "the free disposition and use of tools for a specific end product is replaced by rhythmic unification of the laboring body

Figure 5.19 Snowstorm gradually effacing ski tracks.

with its implement, the movement of laboring itself acting as the unifying source" (Arendt, 1998:145). The rhythm of the ground linked to successive views in the area is eternally evolving. Vision is completed in movement, and movement is completed in vision. As Erwin Straus remarks with his notion of *die Ferne*, there is actually no end to the development of perceived space as long as its target is based on the traveller's momentarily fixed but still instantly temporary standpoint (Straus, 1956:408). Movement through the land understood as human labouring and the cycles of nature are endlessly in flux. But the outcome of the reflection on movement, the product of the continued progress, is still an image of the land experienced in some liminal events, uttered and shared through some distinct motifs.

The ever-shifting ground and the ever-shifting screens of vegetation compose a visual diversity and richness in the area. The cycle of the seasons offers both different ground surface qualities and varying degrees of vegetation transparency. Especially the changes in the ground are acutely felt by the proceeding individual. The friction of the organism, the unit of body, ground and vehicle, differs enormously through the seasons. Occasionally, in wintertime, huge masses of snow render almost impossible any advance into the area (Figure 5.20). Then, following an occasional period of mild weather, the same masses of snow become as solid as a concrete floor, and suddenly movement in all directions is possible, even regardless of equipment, skis or boots. The experienced friction of the organism, the organic *moment*

Figure 5.20 Huge masses of snow.

(Fiskevold, 2011:32), is left as a visible track on the surface of the earth. Regardless of their temporality as a ski track or a tiny path, the traces are not so much an outcome of *work* as of the instantaneous engagement with land through labouring movement. These traces are not so much a product of an idea of where to walk as they are of instant sights and physical negotiations between body and ground. Both as summer and winter paths, they show the instant variation of friction inherent in the organism. The bends in the path, the revealed stones or obstructing trunks, rivers or bogs, each represent a break or continuation, a bodily effort or ease in the act of moving through the land.

During the peak of the winter season some machine-made ski tracks are laid out in the area (Figure 5.21). Though modest in size, they nevertheless introduce current societal ideas about the physical facilitation of movement through the area. Seen as part of *labour*, the road is set out as the controlling agent of the moving body, channelling movement within a zone of restrictions, prescribing or prohibiting certain behaviours. Even the machine tracks through Kustein contain traces of this attitude. Physically, they restrict movement to a tiny corridor through the area. The route is rendered on maps, and listed on a website where the public is informed daily about the current state of the track. Movement across the land is fundamentally easier when travelling in the tracks. The skier no longer has to choose the direction of his or her next move, and snow friction is decisively removed. The

Figure 5.21 Ski track in sunny weather.

standardisation of the surface does not remove the experiences of moving uphill or downhill, of course, but it levels the route, making the transitions less apparent and the right of way more predictable. Moreover, the machine-made track and its way of facilitating movement are influenced by the general idea of public safety. The icy surface of small tarns and some moors are avoided by the machine's driver, thereby avoiding predictable hazards but at the same time diminishing the advantages of movement in wintertime.

The motifs of the human-made path and the machine-made ski tracks accentuate the small transitions which lead the travelling human into or away from a societal and standardised version of movement. The transitions are experienced when the skier leaves or enters the tracks to or from the surrounding ground. They are experienced when the snow melts and the tracks vanish. But they could be experienced in much the same way in the transition from any road which is primarily the result of a design manual as opposed to one that follows the naturally shaped surface of the ground. The elimination of friction is one of the main aims of any road manual. Friction, in contrast, is the fundamental way of experiencing qualitative richness along a route. Areas like Kustein, where the traces of human society are rather modest, still offer the rambler an opportunity to explore the organic diversity of the landscape. Although it is protected by law, it is as though distance alone – the hours of walk and the steep ascent up to the high summit – guarantees the imagery a kind of protection. Separated from the habits of everyday life, the imagery is left unspoilt by intrusions from procedures, budgets and deadlines.

Emancipation: visualising the performance of the organism

Even in areas like Kustein, there are traces of the mindset that influences the way modern travelling takes place. The programming of our movement and travels is omnipresent. The overall goal is for you to survive or avoid heavy injuries when you decide to head off for the post office, the office, school or even the nearby wilderness, on foot or in a car. As the entropy of awareness caused by the omnipresence of virtual reality affects more and more places, and as the expansion of the ensuing non-places increasingly isolates the traveller from the area in which he or she is moving, the impact of the ground on the traveller and the impact of the traveller on the ground are abolished. Human *labour*, in terms of moving through the land, is reduced to the performance of a software-directed journey. The pastoral landscape motif exists as an alternative to this programmed everyday life. The pastoral motifs are contingent on the conventionality of ordinary perceptions, but they appear as visual expansions of what can be expected under ordinary circumstances. In this way, sustaining the diversity of land means resisting, challenging and complementing the influence of modelled and programmed movement.

Entering the roadless area of Kustein means leaving the tracks and routes of civilisation. Guiding signposts and earthworks gradually vanish, subjective engagement and evaluation gradually taking over instead. Proceeding towards a black spot in the otherwise light grey and dark white snow-covered surface, we soon recognise running water. The risk of breaking the snow surface is avoided by occasionally straying off the track. Reflecting upon this modest event, we cannot point at any experience that is *not* participating in the movement through the land. And we cannot single out the decisive moment which prepared our next move. The last step, as well as those taken years ago, to equal extent provides our body with the ability to carry on, to evaluate and choose; all are outcomes of our acting as a part of the present organism. Regardless of the material conditions offered by the area, the success of the journey is critically linked to our subsumed experience and present partaking in the available organism. The rugged branches of the trees deny our body easy access through the same woods that are so easily traversed in summertime; and the snow-covered, undulating ground becomes a predictable floor, offering routes in all directions (Figure 5.22). Summer obstructions such as lakes, rivers and moors have turned into gentle and preferable passage ways. The image that emerges in extension of the person's bodily *labour* (walking or skiing) reflects his or her involvement and skill in finding his or her way in this roadless area. Travellers have to perform bodily adaptations to the ever-changing surface in order to find their

Figure 5.22 Snow transforms the forest ground into a floor.

way through the land. The lack of standardised procedures, the standing need to make decisions based on one's own experience, sets free subjective skills and responsibility. The motif is a pastoral, because it triggers bodily *labour* as involvement in the larger organism of the earth which is *not* under human control or surveillance, and which implies neither expectations nor promises. However, it cannot be perceived without personal involvement. Being involved means being observant of the area's various qualities *there and then* and being able to imagine its latent potential as a route.

The material contribution to the visual evaluation of the ground might be weak or strong. But even when one's judgement fails and the ground no longer carries the traveller, the presence of the organism is no less apparent. On the contrary, the motif of the broken ice surface points to the subjective temporality and terrestrial fragility of the organic landscape. As *labour*, the only means to re-experience this landscape is to repeat the journey as it is provided by the organism. In this organism, the individual is both a transformer of the ground and a receiver of the land. Every step constitutes the individual in a unique engagement with the organism. The terrestrial fragility of the engagement, the perceived event of the ongoing movement, the ever-shifting horizon and the fleeting processes of nature, both set an end to and mark the beginning of labour partaking in the land as landscape. Each actual move of the body simultaneously closes the formerly open array of potential moves. Any decision leaves but one

Figure 5.23 Logging machine.

imprint on the chosen piece of land. Any spot that we carefully examined as a potential way of proceeding is suddenly wiped out of relevance as well as memory. Of all the richness of the route, there is not much left of the trip in terms of remembered images. The image of the area consists of fragments of the route. The motif reveals how the virgin area allows the rambler to see him- or herself as a transitory part of nature's many instances and cycles. Terrestrial fragility and subjective temporality are but two sides of the same coin.

The awareness of fragility is, however, another way to intensify the engagement with land. Remembering the logging machine, we immediately fear that the forest scene might vanish at any time (Figure 5.23). The next time we visit the area, it may have been cleared. The knowledge of this possibility affects our perception of the area. It is as though we are leaving the image wherever we look. Will we meet the old spruce next time we walk on this track? Or will it have been transformed into a newspaper sheet, or into building material somewhere? The value of the image may increase through this knowledge. It is as though we are looking at the passing scenes as exceptional events. At the very moment we become aware of them, present in shape and substance, we see them disappear, removed by the imagined logging machine. Then, shutting our eyes, we realise that we are situated in the middle of a nature reserve. The growth which surrounds us is temporarily protected from the programme of the budget, or the jaws of the machine. Though we are aware of the temporality of everything, from reserve to regulation, we still recognise the pragmatism of civilisation. We know that the next time we visit the area, the chances are high that we may recognise the scenes that we are leaving now. Our perception resides in the knowledge of the area's status as a nature reserve, although our image of it derives from the repeated scenes of trees, moss and moors.

Land reflected as landscapes

Landscapes are objects of analysis, and motifs are products of the analyst's attention and *action*. Our demonstration of contemporary pastoral landscape motifs, narrated as articulated, material or organic landscapes, has revealed the fundamental connection between human activity and land visualised as landscapes. We have shown that a pastoral landscape motif is far more than a property of the land. Moreover, the motifs are outcomes of common and shared practices of travel which are interpreted analytically in accordance with a pastoral tradition. Although their key component differs, they are all conceptually guided elaborations of ideas.

Organic reactions, material resistance and articulated responses materialised in pastoral landscape motifs

First, pastoral landscapes can draw on the acting person's reflection upon the very concept of landscape itself. A discursive *action*, an imaginative *response* (Cassirer, 1944:27) then mirrors the landscape as an object of evaluation according to environmental or other policies. The development of arguments in the narrative, the partaking in discussions and the commitment to conclusions develops the land into landscapes that are an outcome of a plurality of human modes of action, but seen from a clearly articulated, pastoral value perspective. In terms of *action*, our object of investigation, the road, is part of a public discourse, an arena for different decision makers such as politicians, public managers, planners and lobbyists. As an outcome of *action*, the scene of the road displays a multitude of intentions, projects and prospects, which partly coincide with and partly oppose those of the transport bureaucracy or other powerful driving forces. The *action* of the analyst therefore means the articulation of the ideal of human-nature unity in the land, an *articulated landscape*, not simply in the medium but as the decisive argument of speech. The key component of the *articulated landscape* is revealed in the linguistic utterance itself and can be legitimised neither in the material character nor in the bodily reception of the surface of land. In the construction of this landscape, the analyst emphasises the road environment's significance as humanity-nature unity, in response to the road as a landscape of power.

Second, a landscape pastoral can draw on the analyst's attention to the land as *created objects*. The permanence and durability in human *work* represents a material confrontation with and *resistance to* natural erosion and decay. The objective human imprints on the surface of the land appear as a *material landscape*. Pastoral motifs are then visualisations of material resistance to and from the land itself and testify to the analyst's capacity to articulate a symbolic image of it, displayed through the specific character of the site. In terms of *work*, the road appears as a *model* for altering the land in order to resist those natural forces which obstruct smooth and predictable transportation. As *work*, the road represents an objectification of those human evaluations, decisions and practices that can be proclaimed as essential for the utility of the road. The *action* of the analyst therefore means the visualisation of the humanity-nature unity as a resistance to constant material changes.

Finally, a landscape pastoral motif can be drawn from a person's bodily experience. The human body's impulsive *reactions* (Cassirer, 1944:27), nevertheless, are not confined to the body as organism. The materiality of the actual land equally has a share in landscape perception, as human *labour* in the land extends perception into that of an *organic landscape*. The corresponding motifs are visualisations of organic movement through the land and testify to the analyst's capacity to articulate these symbolically with reference to defined, experienced sequences of motion. In terms of *labour*, the road provides a defined site for human *movement* on land. Thus, movement does not sprawl randomly as if in an open field, but is staged as scenes and sequences along a right of way and standardised through the technical properties of any available and authorised vehicle.

The mutual interdependency of articulated, material and organic landscapes

The relation between human practices and the visibility of motifs, that is, their capacity to be shared, cannot be attributed unconditionally to a location. The materialisation of pastoral motifs follows utterances *about*, not single features *in* an area. Even though they have been picked out here for the exemplary illustration of articulated, material and organic landscapes, the respective sites of Edelgranveien, Vækerø and Kustein could equally have been presented in other landscape versions.

The road of Edelgranveien, analysed as an instance of the modern pastoral landscape, may also lead to other aesthetic events and reflections on material as well as organic landscape motifs. As an outcome of *work*, as material landscape, the road is part of an ideological model. It is made for predictability, efficiency and order. As an outcome of *labour*, as organic landscape, the road is occasionally removed from the permanence and durability of the model. The prescribed corridor for pedestrians can be blocked by a snowfall, or the pavement be removed for repair work. As in Kustein, we are

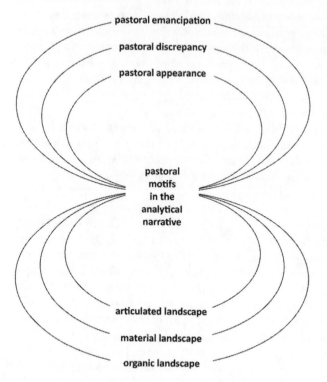

Figure 5.24 Pastoral motives and landscapes of reflection condense and separate in the motifs of a narrative.

then required to mobilise our experience and rely on our own judgement to negotiate the situation.

The estate at Vækerø, which we analysed as an instance of the landscape as human *work* – that is, for its contribution to understanding the physical character of the land as a pastoral motif – also provides possible visualisations of articulated as well as organic landscape motifs. As an outcome of *action*, that is, as articulated landscape, the area may be visualised through several different rhetorical approaches to land as landscape. The verbal response to the land could be exemplified in the actions which preceded the layout of the park at the end of the 1800s, in the construction of the motorway in the 1950s, and in the development of the western part of the park into an office complex in the 1980s and 2000s. As an outcome of *labour*, as organic landscape, the site's location adjacent to the Oslo fjord shows the natural cycles of tide and sky mirrored on the sea's surface; and in the short periods in winter when snow covers the lawn for maybe a day or two, it may be visualised as enabling skiers to play on the small piece of land.

The area of Kustein, which we have analysed as an instance of the accidental presence of the organism, may also provide visualisations of articulated as well as material landscape motifs. As an outcome of *action*, as articulated landscape, the area visualises the values of nature preservation, both those that were applied when the nature reserve was established in 1991 and those when it was extended in 2016. As an outcome of *work*, as material landscape, the area is made part of a model landscape which works to legitimise the area's outstanding values as providing a sense of humanity-nature unity. This model in turn is an outcome of the act of nature preservation. Making the area into a nature reserve simultaneously puts an end to the influence of the management model of forestry.

Giving visibility to an evolving world

The interdependencies and special characteristics of the articulated, material and organic landscapes affect the landscape analysis in all sorts of ways. Regarding the landscape analytical approach as *action* and utterance, and in doing so emphasising the rhetorical aspect of landscape pastorals, an analysis is nevertheless documented in reports and thus transformed into *work*. Consequently, the reading of these documents must be related to the readers' experiences achieved by *labour*, experiencing the world. When we are moving through the woods near Kustein, the organic landscape emerges into appearance. When we are imagining time periods at Vækerø, it is the material landscape which makes the foreground. When we are conceptually framing the everyday road of Edelgranveien, it is the articulated landscape which is materialised and narrated in visible motifs. But when these experiences and imaginings are articulated and shared as a narrative, the sensation of land is inevitably replaced by the unity of the symbolic image. Moreover, when we as analysts or people make these landscapes emerge into appearance as visible motifs, they are framed by and transformed into verbal images.

Without denying the material impact on landscape formation, we have seen that landscapes are born, nurtured and protected by language. The pastoral landscape motifs which we have just articulated *are* the landscapes of Edelgranveien, Vækerø and Kustein to the readers of this book. Landscapes in the meaning of symbolic images cannot exist without a unifying idea which makes parts of the evolving world visible for an attentive reader or listener. Only after being told and comprehended are they attached to a piece of land, explained as a feature, associated with a moral standard or (as emphasised in this book) with one of the three fundamental activities corresponding to the basic conditions "under which life on earth has been given to man" (Arendt, 1998:7).

Thus, although the analytical narrative represents real aspects of land, it totally presents and thereby creates perceptions of an area, a humanity-nature relationship, namely landscapes. The motivation to let landscapes emerge into appearance is as old as the pastoral tradition itself. Looking at the *Eclogues* from different conceptual perspectives, Saunders is struck by how they "conceive of the literary tradition as a world they not only inherit and inhabit, but also redefine and reorder" (Saunders, 2008:60). One way of tracing this reordering is to notice how the landscape utterance tends to draw attention to the performativity of the utterance itself, that is, how the analytical narrative helps to make the human relation to land visible as landscape. The purpose of any pastoral landscape analysis is to present motifs and propose ideas of humanity-nature unity. Our proposed idylls of Edelgranveien, Vækerø and Kustein may seem conservative and outdated, but the way they have come into being is still essentially tied to the contemporary world. They may therefore still have their relevance in an increasingly computerised society.

References

Arendt, H. 1978. *The life of the mind*, San Diego, Harcourt.
Arendt, H. 1998. *The human condition*, Chicago, University of Chicago Press.
Bakhtin, M. 2006. *The dialogic imagination: four essays*, Austin, University of Texas Press.
Borden, I. 2012. *Drive: journeys through film, cities and landscapes*, London, Reaktion.
Cassirer, E. 1944. *An essay on man: an introduction to a philosophy of human culture*, New Haven, Yale University Press.
Egebjerg, U. & Simonsen, P. 2005. *Byen, vejen og landskabet: motorveje til fremtiden*, Aalborg, Aalborg universitet.
Featherstone, M., Thrift, N. & Urry, J. 2005. *Automobilities*, London, Sage.
Fiskevold, M. 2011. *Veien som vilje og forestilling: analysemetoder for landskap og estetisk erfaring*, Ås, Universitetet for miljø- og biovitenskap.
Friedlander, L. 2010. *America by car*, New York, DAP.
Graf, c. 2013. *Der fotografische Essay: ein Hybrid aus Bild, Text und Film*, München, Wilhelm Fink.
Jackson, J. B. 1994. *A sense of place, a sense of time*, New Haven, Yale University Press.
Latour, B. 2005. *Reassembling the social: an introduction to actor-network-theory*, New York, Oxford University Press.
Morrison, K. & Minnis, J. 2013. *Carscapes: the motor car, architecture and landscape in England*, New Haven, Yale University Press.
Panofsky, E. 1982. *Meaning in the visual arts*, Chicago, University of Chicago Press.
Saunders, T. 2008. *Bucolic ecology: Virgil's* Eclogues *and the environmental literary tradition*, London, Duckworth.
Straus, E. 1956. *Vom Sinn der Sinne: ein Beitrag zur Grundlegung der Psychologie*, Berlin, Springer.
Urry, J. 2007. *Mobilities*, Cambridge, Polity.
Zeller, T. 2007. *Driving Germany: the landscape of the German autobahn, 1930–1970*, New York, Berghahn Books.

Chapter 6

The landscape analyst's
pastoral *action*

Computed landscapes

From the mechanics of machines to society's software programs

The modern road's programmes represent but one version of the widespread reduction of human life to commodified quantities, which we have identified as disempowerment and counterforce in the pastoral tradition. Where Marx referred to the "machine" in the garden, what we meet today in the garden are society's "software programs". However, while the machine was, and still is, a material object leaving visible traces on the ground, software runs silently in the background of human life, its programmed logics greatly influencing the surface of the earth, but without necessarily leaving any traceable imprints on it. The very invisibility of powerful decision makers is increasingly modifying the activities and attitudes of contemporary societies. The computerisation of human life and human thinking is performed as incessant transactions of data, offering us a virtual world that is conceived through simulacra (Baudrillard, 2007:36). In a recent debate in the *Frankfurter Allgemeine Zeitung* (Schirrmacher, 2015b), this tendency and its implications are elaborated on. When we operate a laptop or a smartphone, through our own trivial contributions, e.g. ordering a bus ticket, we confirm the programmers' presumptions, and our own speech is replaced by algorithmic thoughts. The categories and behaviour we are offered by the programmers through their software also work the other way round: they shape our attitudes in such a way that we gradually become copies of digital thoughts (Yogeshwar, 2015:83–84, our translation):

> They [computer systems] apply methods in order to be able to read our properties, they image us as digital profile; and without noticing, we start to correspond to [...] their categories. We silently accept that a human is being reduced to the sum of his or her measurable properties, that is, becomes a digital object.

In sum, even our thinking becomes automatised (Baum, 2015:56).

The invisible infrastructure of monitoring

More than 30 years ago, Lyotard was quite aware of the possible outcomes of a computerised society. As he predicted, the system "could become the 'dream' instrument for controlling and regulating the market system, extended to include knowledge itself and governed exclusively by the performativity principle" (Lyotard, 1984:67). Today, scarcely anyone carrying out a Google search is provoked by the advertisements that pop up as a result of the instant scanning of our actions that is carried out by the search engine. This invisible infrastructure, which is designed to monitor human activity, silently records your journeys and, unnoticed, tries to impact on your future choices (Zuboff, 2015:178). The owners and developers of software take possession both of individuals' clicks as data *and* of the context in which these clicks belong (the market of information). Providing a platform for interaction is just a part of the digital infrastructure. What is even more valuable is to master the right to make interpretations of the data and trigger their labouring activity among humans. The invisible digital infrastructure is often designed in such a way as to make it seem as if decisions belong to the individual. The software for modern cars, for example, is always promoted as driver assistance systems. But instead of "assisting" the driver, the system also enables him or her to pay less attention to the road environment. Although on the one hand representing an advantage, the systems also simultaneously reduce the driver's role as the one in charge, and his or her skills of awareness of the land crossed. The invisible infrastructure withdraws the drivers from the condition of *action* and engulfs them as data and as *part* of the *labouring* software of society. As a result, the individual skill to experience and master nature as landscape, in both its hostile and its delightful versions, gradually decays. Even walking out of one's front door may appear unsafe, or as the opposite: *images* of the Norwegian tourist hotspots Prekestolen (Pulpit Rock) and Trolltunga (Troll Tongue) draw crowds of hikers, but their understanding of the posted images' reality is often revealed as lacking when local Red Cross volunteers rescue frozen and exhausted tourists from their own enterprise. The script promises an extraordinary selfie but does not take into account the skills that are required to carry out the exhausting hike. In the computerised landscapes of social media, the selfie moment is multiplied among all who are capable of understanding its social-web reality, but regardless, alas, of their incapability of grasping its physical reality.

The elimination of analytical critique through digital landscaping strategies

The flow of data imitating the life-sustaining processes of *labour* is further strengthened by the activities and sustenance of landscape planning in modern bureaucracies. The principle of the Norwegian roads administration's "zero vision", for instance – the goal of zero fatal accidents on Norwegian roads – although easily laudable in itself, directs large proportions of surplus resources into technical installations and construction manuals that transmit the idea that one's highest achievement in life is to stay alive. It conceptualises travel as an uninterrupted flow of predicted occurrences, and it frames how we speak, act and resign ourselves to the ways in which our daily movements are steered. This happens at the cost of the ideal that each individual should grasp whatever opportunities there are to "make a difference" (*action*), which *do* present themselves to a historically unprecedented degree in modern democratic societies.

The landscape concept's liminality between environmental management's horizon of efficiency and the pastoral idea can resist this breakdown into *labour* only on condition that the tension between positive and negative ideals is kept active. If not, the dissolution of landscape into data for *efficient labour*, the infinite repetition of standardised procedures of planning and resource management techniques, lies as a latent threat within the analytical landscape utterance itself. We finally find our professional as well as individual freedom lost in a society's expectations where the human activities of *action* and *work* have been totally replaced by *labour*, circulating "a 'natural force', the force of the life process itself" (Arendt, 1998:321).

This becomes apparent in the use of the map. In this process, however, the human awareness of nature and the *action* of choosing representational means, as shown in the map as *work*, are constantly threatened by the efficiency of standardisation, which reduces action and work to *labour*. The map facilitates calculations and equations all over the world according to its own rules of operation. The map renders the land as properties (resources) and prepares it for human use independently of its material and symbolic presence at any given moment in time and place. Once broken down into spatial entities, so appealing to the map and the mapping mentality, the original idea of landscape is most effectively disarmed and relegated to the background. Analytical subdivision replaces the synthesising force of motifs, whose relevance as indicators must be constantly and explicitly reconsidered as the landscape is reinterpreted. A comprehensive mapping of the mainland of Norway as "landscape" is currently being finalised as part of the large Nature in Norway (NiN) project (Erikstad et al., 2013). The work is based on an early mapping test which was carried out in the county of Nordland. One of the aims of this project has been to make the outcomes of analysing landscapes less observer-dependent, that is, more value-neutral. A great quantity of data from different databases, and their calculation and compilation into various land categories, make for the answer to this challenge. The project demonstrates how the choices and evaluations made – for instance, of databases and their interrelation and priority – all of which of course are results of human *action*, are removed from public criticism. NiN's computerised landscape hides the traces of the programmers' selections behind the myth of data systems' and software's neutrality. Computed landscape maps preclude any transparent and meaningful gathering of essentially useful data, for *different* possible and explicitly stated purposes. With time, we might even start limiting our very thinking to the confines of the model. This new landscape will predetermine our way of thinking about as well as imaging the face of the country.

The desire for replicability and efficiency neutralises landscape analysis as a human action

The computed landscape is one of the recent spinoffs of modern technological progress, which has both liberated and troubled modern humanity for centuries. When it is applied to the practice of analysing landscapes, we recognise with Heidegger (Heidegger, 1996:86) that modern technique is potentially more devastating to human thought than to life on earth. In chapter two we saw how the once symbolic imaging of landscapes has gradually been reduced to the mere documentation of properties of land in contemporary planning. In the assessment of the performativity of a landscape analysis method, the idea of efficiency has been prioritised over the tradition of *reflective visualisation* of humans' ongoing dealings with nature. Seeming resemblances between nature and its representation through tools blur the distinction between nature and human artifice. Ortega y Gasset, cited by Marx, commented on how people seemed to receive the motor cycle as a natural force (Marx, 2000:7). Almost a hundred years later, the same instinct-like reception seems to be the case concerning digital information systems and media (Schirrmacher, 2015a:63). However, contrary to nature, which always appears as a rebirth and variation of itself, technology presupposes predictability and produces sameness. By transferring the *labour* of nature onto the *work* of technology, society has evolved, much as Arendt predicted, in a uniform and *action*-reluctant direction (Arendt, 1998:40):

> It is decisive that society, on all its levels, excludes the possibility of action [...]. Instead, society expects from each of its members a certain kind of behavior, imposing innumerable and various rules, all of which tend to "normalize" its members, to make them behave, to exclude spontaneous action or outstanding achievement.

Any attempt to conceive human *action* as an item of data, whether it is people's perceptions or the characteristics of the land, easily draws our attention away from how a landscape always emerges into appearance as an event of there and then. The utopian desire to map all the "landscape characters" of a country's territory, or to extract a biological truth behind people's preference for particular scenery, distracts the landscape analyst from his or her extraordinary task: giving the world a visible, comprehensible and potentially pleasurable shape. The almost authoritarian insistence on a value-free, objective observation of the physical world makes landscapes less visible. The worlds of selfies, maps and statistics are united in being expressed in "likes", "polygons" or "numbers" which make sense only if the goal is efficient consumption and control. Sustaining efficiency means that these systems' landscaping customers, whether they are labelled "tourists", "analysts" or "planners", must react with appropriate *labour*. Any reflective *action* must be given up when we, programmers included, can no longer oversee the consequences of choices that are made by a handful of powerful people. In Arendt's terms, it is the plurality of the world which is at stake when *labouring* systems threaten to wipe out the last remnant of visible connections between experience and knowledge. If that connection – that is, the very motivation for seeing landscapes – is to be restored and maintained, practitioners of landscape analysis should become more aware of their pastoral heritage.

The visual rationality of analytical narratives

In a move towards making a blurred world stand out as distinct and visible, we have emphasised that the analyst has to fix, select and arrange parts of the visible world as a *motif*. Whether the motif *materialises* through a poem's words, in a painting's pigments or in a landscape analysis, it always requires a certain configuration which is a combination of a human thought and an environment. Consequently, the analysis must show how any present *potential* for a piece of land to be transformed into a landscape depends on a dual horizon. *Seljefløiten*, for example, was created neither out of necessity nor accidentally. The painting owes its existence to both the horizon of the painter's motion *in* the area and the horizon of his comprehension *of* the area. It presupposed a knowledge of the physical traits of the area and of how to reach the particular location; but it also presupposed a certain artistic trend which made Skredsvig, a member of the Fleskum circle of artists, explore the land and show it in this particular version. Finally, the analytical utterance is completed in its *realisation* as an *image* of the land as landscape.

Landscape awareness exposed and evoked by the voice of the analyst

In *Arcadia updated* we have elaborated on how analytical narratives can raise landscape awareness. Starting with classical pastoral works, we have identified the three motives of *emergence into appearance*, *discrepancy* and *emancipation*. We have let these motives guide us through the existential situation of the landscape analyst (chapter three), let them highlight analytical narration as a possibility in public decision-making processes (chapter

four), and finally (chapter five) let them guide the articulation of three contemporary pastoral landscape drafts. Through all these different approaches,
we have argued that the only way to sustain landscapes' poetic potential is
to have confidence in the endurance of pastoral landscape vision as a way
for modern humans to negotiate their existential liminality as earthly beings.

In the example from Vegaøyan, we saw that landscapes, as opposed to
areas, are a property not of the land but of seeing the land as landscape.
The World Heritage landscape of eider down harvesting on the Vega Islands
does not accrue from the area's material features alone, but is founded on
an institutionalised interpretation of them which designates them as parts of
a site of universal and outstanding value. Landscapes, however impressive
they appear, do not emerge into appearance unless rocks and villages, trees
and rivers are united in an analytical narrative about them, which subsequently becomes a visual guide for seeing.

Accepting existing narratives as important references for analysing
landscapes, we saw in the examples from Telemark and Sarpefossen that
pastoral liminality is not limited to the object of the analysis, the landscape,
but is inherent in the design of the analytical method itself. From a methodological point of view, the dialectic between a negative ideal and a positive ideal is paralleled by the dialectic between the poetic potential of an
analytical utterance (*action*) on the positive side and its goals of replicability
(as *work*) and efficiency (for *labour*) on the negative side. While an analytical narrative makes landscapes available for shared awareness, the analytical narrative's own design defines its opportunity to deal with its intended
object.

Landscapes are perceived and experienced anywhere and by anyone. But
as the example from Storhei shows, it is the analyst who has the specialist's
competence to articulate vision through language. Creating landscapes,
keeping them relevant through time, and making them fit for public discourse with analytical narratives thus raises landscape awareness across
districts and nations. Landscape analysts should cultivate their skill for
assembling material memories, cultural values and imagined proposals into
coherently reflecting utterances.

Reflecting the pastoral motivation of the analytical narrative, we left
institutionalised methodology and continued our investigation of landscapes
as objects of analysis, following the premises of pastoral narration. In the
organic sensing of Kustein, in the perception of Vækerø as artefact, and in
the rhetorical visualisation of the concept of Edelgranveien, we were able to
identify material motifs that manifest human perception in the conditions
of *labour*, *work* and *action* respectively. In these pastoral drafts, we pointed
to an alternative to the mainstream procedures of characterisation that are
connected to maps and predefined area properties. Although they differ in
scope and complexity, all these landscapes, without exception, as analytical
narratives are instances of human *action*.

Contemporary landscapes become visible through pastoral action

Being part of public decision-making processes, the practice of analysing landscapes implies taking a political stance in a world between an evolving nature and humanity's recurrent imagining of a nature. In activating the relation between land and humanity as organic, material and articulated reflection, analytical narratives propose a constructive, dialectical and revelatory act of seeing which complements whatever existing models enhance humanity's consumptive approach to land. Both for the analysts and for the people who are affected by an analysis, the strategy of analytical narration provides a chance to step out of society's instrumental schemes, be they the computations of the tourist industry and planning departments or the paradigms of science. *Action* means suspending society's conventional narratives and engaging with temporary tasks and immediate incidents. *Action*, the essential part of what constitutes any relevant landscape perception, is left out of the scope of modern technique, as Heidegger (Heidegger, 1996) suggests. But similarly to Ritter (Ritter, 1974), he also concludes that modern technique cannot destroy humans' imagination and their capability to perceive the richness of the world that lies beyond the limits of techniques. Any attempt to deal with the evolving world technologically, that is, to make it fit for calculation, replication and prediction, will always provoke an alternative to emerge into appearance.

In a world that increasingly produces, relies on and believes in the *simulacra* of a virtual reality, it is precisely human *action* which should be the analytical narrative's intentional point of departure. Human *action* is what modern technique tries to minimise, and should therefore be what the analytical narrative accentuates. Accepting *action* as the fundamental constituent of any landscape analysis, our strategy should be to direct our attention towards developing analytical narratives. Two fundamental requirements must be met. Firstly, in motifs that are visible for everyone, the analytical narrative must materialise the meaning content of contemporary landscapes. Through pastoral motives, the analyst must transform the sight of a piece of land into an insight about a landscape. Secondly, the analyst should locate the narrative's motifs within a horizon of motion as well as one of comprehension in order to give them legitimacy. As *narrative action*, the analysis must leave behind any ambition of mastering the land, whether through controlling its features or gaining an overview of people's preferences. Rather, it should rely on present images of an evolving nature, as perceived by engaged subjects.

Updated pastoral motifs and the potential for restorative vision

Against a horizon of ongoing change, a landscape analysis says something about how we can evaluate an area's *potential* as landscape (Fiskevold,

2016; Stahlschmidt et al., 2017). With reference to a pastoral ideal, the practice of analysing landscapes bears witness to humans' present engagement with land. It is the analyst – according to the Landscape Convention an expert – who should raise landscape awareness by giving this engagement visible form in presented motifs. The aim of a landscape analysis, therefore, can be neither to avoid idealisation nor to contribute to efficient manuals or guidelines, but instead to clarify what its ideal vision implies. Like Meliboeus in *Eclogue* 1, he or she must visualise what Tityrus is not capable of seeing. Thus, landscape analyses should not limit their field of action to inventorying and producing statistics or maps, but should additionally seek to explain and reshape the way we see and evaluate those activities. The analysis must demonstrate the importance of looking, seeing and reflecting on what one *sees* as indispensable for understanding and knowing.

The challenge for the analyst is to demonstrate the reciprocity and complementary function of both negative and positive pastoral ideals. The seeming idyll is only ever idyllic as long as it is seen *in relation to* a negatively perceived aspect of reality to which the protagonists of a poem or a narrative draw attention, be it the loss of a homestead (as in Vergil's first *Eclogue*), the loss of a lover or concern over some environmental degradation. As we demonstrated in our own account, it is not until the value of Dælivannet is realised as a counterforce to the sprawl of housing estates and daily commutes to the city and shopping centres that we can appreciate fully the meaning of the picnic area by the lake. In Hiltner's words, "by placing the reader in the liminal space between emerging and receding backdrops [the analyst] is able to draws attention to both" (Hiltner, 2011:45). Not until we see the images at Kustein as a negation of the standardised urban road, not until we are capable of recognising the temporariness of the motorway scene in contrast to the permanence of the fjord at Vækerø, and not until we admit the infinitude of potentially emerging pastoral landscape versions along our regular journey on Edelgranveien do we realise the influence of both a shared poetic inheritance and a possibly common human sensing of the site.

The landscapes we presented of Edelgranveien, Vækerø and Kustein are all outcomes of an understanding of contemporary society. As we pointed to through our chosen motifs, the landscapes in these areas are visual reflections of a human condition. These motifs gesture at meaningful landscapes, symbolic of contemporary humanity-nature relationships. Both their literal description and their societal background tell us something about the state of the world. However, in the shift of horizons provided by the analytical narratives, they manage to display a transaction between virtual and organic realities. In attaching motifs to an activity that is carried out within a horizon of motion, the reader is drawn into the liminal space between landscapes of *labour, work* and *action*. As stressed throughout this book, the restorative outcome of this evaluative activity is strictly dependent on the analyst's subjective ability to take advantage of the gap between tangible and intangible references in the design of the analytical narrative itself.

Meliboeus' ability to link the sight of his native land to his insight into the workings of societal power and injustice is simultaneously his way out of his existential dilemma as well as the dilemma of the confrontation with Tityrus. Meliboeus reconciles himself to his fate by oscillating between longing for his former lost life and re-cognising it in the present orchard landscape. At the moment of reconciliation, both his earlier experiences and his knowledge about his present exile are active. Reconciliation does not accrue from histories about past glorious times or future hope. It occurs in a clash between an active man and the worldly actualities that he must confront. Realising that he is expelled from his former way of living (*labour*) and the productive *work* he used to carry out, he finds a solution in making an overview of his situation. His *work* and his *labour* are replaced by *action*. As his material and organic landscapes are no longer attainable, they are replaced by the appearance of an articulated landscape.

The potential for awareness-raising depends on the analysis' references to an outside world

Presenting a landscape by pointing to a motif gives both the analyst and the audience an opportunity to expand and deepen their own sense of reality and being. The *narrative* part of a landscape utterance is always shared by analyst and audience. As Walter Benjamin once stated, the narrator's aim is to make the listener into his or her successor, that is, to make the listeners or readers into narrators themselves (Benjamin, 1991:443). Landscapes can settle down in another individual and thus expand their narrative field of action. *Narrating* an analysis means performing transactions between invisible subjective ideas and images through visible motifs. The images themselves, however, are out of reach of analytical narration's objectification. Subjective imagination, invisible to others, should be permitted to stay that way. It cannot be replaced by anything visible. The analyst has to rely on an imaginative receiver, that is, a presumably attentive listener, who may or may not exist.

Pastoral *action* means relying on external references such as other people's imagination of the world. The potential for imagination to be shared between analyst and audience, however, is subject to an ever-evolving and only partially controllable nature, as well as to societal conventions and values. Pastoral *action* means accepting the unavoidable confrontations with the world inherent in its *liminal* position. We have seen that Meliboeus' strength lies in his being able to reflect on his former life, thereby giving his present life a meaning, purpose and reference, in opposition to society's exertion of power over him. The restorative potential of pastoral *action* is dependent on a world which, like nature or society, is beyond individual control. The restorative potential of the pastoral attitude depends on an individual's ongoing as well as immediate relating to the world's temporality, that is, a self-*emplacement* in relation to it. When this constitutive, self-conscious emplacement of the self outside of the flow of time and space is disrupted, the restorative potential of the pastoral is similarly put to an end: "At this point, nature loses all restorative potential through alliance with the chaos of human experience. No objective standards measure the lover's vision of nature; his only measure is himself" (Leach, 1974:158). When human ideals, positive or negative, are derived purely from ideology or opaque calculations, nature is dismissed as a corrective force. Any unpleasant confrontation with reality is replaced by the common inclinations to wishful thinking, sentimental longing, blind trust or obedience. As we argued in the previous chapter, the ever-increasing programming of travel that materialises in the road is one of the symptoms of this tendency. Manuals for landscape assessment and road-planning directives draw their legitimacy from a certain way of compiling data, which is mistaken for a true representation of the objectively existing world. However, as all external references to concrete human experiences are increasingly set aside, the program, sooner or later, will produce mere circular arguments, landscapes that are a collection of positive ideals. Far from representing landscapes, they effectuate the idea that the abstract means of technology can represent land as landscape in an adequate way. The *work* they produce is the *hardscapes* of computing society, not *landscapes* of human experience and perception. When landscapes are isolated as computable data, the link between the voice of the analyst and the eye of the listener is broken. A *polis of the eye*, an arena for critical exchange, can never be established. Only a non-articulated and non-modelled nature may serve as a reference according to which people can adjust their course of life.

Following a pastoral attitude, the task of reconfiguring and renewing landscapes is not meant to be accomplished. The analytical narrative has to "leap the fence" of earlier landscape *work* and *labour*, always keeping in mind that motifs are temporary visions of the world's ever upcoming events and tasks. Pastoral *action* accepts the complexities of the world as well as human efforts to clear up the disorder of things. Like the tune in the poem that introduced this book, no landscape is present on demand. Even as the tune reaches the boy's ear and attracts his attention, it fades away from immediate sensation. If the tune should suddenly re-enter the boy's sensation, it will be as a memory, even for him. As the Lord's voice clearly reminds us, the tune presents itself as a friend, not as an object that can be possessed. Or, as Winsor Leach concludes, "[t]his failure to satisfy the same longings that give it birth is, in fact, the major source of complexity in pastoral" (Leach, 1974:176). The aesthetic act of landscape perception and communication, taken seriously as such, will never reproduce its results.

An analysis is a process of objectification, but it is the objectification of an insight, an insight which can never be final. No area is ever analysed as landscape once and for all. The frustration fed by the inability to articulate a final answer or to propose a universal solution to a problem may still get its reward through chosen motifs' reinterpretation of old pastoral motives and landscape utterances' success in enlightening us about an evolving nature and world.

Landscape beauty: the analytical narrative's gift to its reader

Arcadia updated has sought to rehabilitate *pastoral action* as a way to raise landscape awareness through the institution of landscape analysis and through the medium of the analytical narrative. In doing this, we have avoided approaches which to varying degrees rely on fixed frameworks, such as methods, maps or categories. In short, we rely on the performativity of an analytical narrative to materialise a visible and shareable motif and present it in either documents (*work*) or meetings (*action*). As we have demonstrated, the analytical narrative strengthens human *action* in two ways: first, the dynamism of any external, worldly reference continuously necessitates reinterpretation; second, the pastoral tradition encodes this reinterpretation with an enduring motivation. In the end, however, neither external references nor the reinterpreting action itself can withstand the utterance that is assembled and stored in the *work*, the analytical narrative itself. As Lyotard admits, "[t]he narratives themselves have this authority. In a sense, the people are only that which actualizes the narratives" (Lyotard, 1984:23). When the analyst has carried out his *action*, evidently, the analytical narrative remains as a piece of *work*. Analytical narratives, in their negotiation of human liminality through the representation of land, remain our only commonly shared approach to conceiving the unity between humanity and nature. In our comprehension of these narratives, a certain beauty emerges into appearance. The American photographer Robert Adams, who is associated with the "New Topographics" exhibition of 1975, articulated this in the following way: "Paradoxically, however, we also need to see the whole geography, natural and man-made, to experience a peace; all land, no matter what has happened to it, has a grace, an absolutely persistent beauty" (Adams, 2008). Like Adams, authors such as John B. Jackson, John Berger, Joachim Ritter, Alain Roger, Eleonor Winsor Leach, Erwin Panofsky and Paul Alpers similarly confess that any land can display beauty. The pastoral strategy of integrating society's disempowering forces as essential background for the foregrounding of some aspect of the land as meaningful landscape acknowledges beauty as something that emerges from the interplay between positive and negative ideals. The German urbanist Thomas Sieverts has characterized this balanced view as *aesthetic sustainability* (Sieverts, 2003:45):

What is experienced negatively as fragmentation and incoherence through the inability to perceive the whole can also be perceived as a high degree of complexity through richness in discontinuities, richness in ecological and social niches and as a subjective spatial enlargement.

Following Ritter (Ritter, 1974), we argue that the aesthetic sustainability of an analytical narrative lies in its capacity to turn an awareness of colliding values and intentions into an insight into human existential liminality: it is an ability to show that human life is in *need* of a reconciliatory attitude. Reconciliation should be the goal of the raised awareness that we seek to achieve through analysing landscapes: reconciliation to the fact that there will always be discrepancies of vision, and to the fact that no final control, no ground zero, can ever be attained.

Consequently, for an analysed landscape to be aesthetically sustainable, the analyst must be willing to enter the world of the Arcadian myth critically and attempt to let it shed light on the present. In order to be aesthetically potent, and thus aesthetically as well as socially sustainable, both the tradition's declaration of limitations and offering of opportunities must be adapted to our own time. In order to complete this ambition, the analytical utterance has to critically investigate not only the land, but also its own performative effect as a current version of the metaphorical design of landscapes. Pastoral *action*, the voice of the analyst, should always keep vital the discrepancy between how we *are expected* to look and the more revealing way in which we *could* look. We must realise that it is the *dialectic* of critical denunciation and acceptance that makes landscapes emerge into appearance. In the act of seeing and showing, the analytical narrative provides a tool both to identify the driving forces of society, visible or hidden, and to propose a complementary act of imagining. Landscape imagination oscillates hermeneutically within a *liminal* space between critique and acceptance. *Pastoral action*, as provided for by the *work* of the analytical narrative, detects contemporary landscapes in both their ordinariness and their outstandingness.

In its best practices, through aesthetic engagement, an analytical narrative may challenge individual world views and raise landscape awareness. Pastoral *liminality* – the manifestation of the dialectic between negative and positive ideals linked to a current human activity – may nurture "human imagination and the home it finds and makes for itself in the world" (Alpers, 1996:65). A space is offered where each person can explore and subsequently take advantage of existing possibilities in life. One way of experiencing the richness of human life is to explore symbolic landscapes like those that we presented of Kustein, Vækerø and Edelgranveien, each reflecting a different aspect of human life conditions. Treated as analytical unities, they present the latency of each individual's freedom to articulate an aesthetically sustainable landscape argument. Landscapes are only sustainable when they are the result of an aesthetic engagement with land. In our opinion, the relation between experts and laypeople can be described neither as a top-down nor a bottom-up relationship. On the contrary, landscape pastorals code it as a side-by-side relationship, in that they rely on our confidence in knowledge, in experience and in imagination. It presumes that both analyst and listener accept a given piece of land as a potentially shared foundation for their identity and insights. In this way, analytical narratives may represent a forward-looking answer to the European Landscape Convention's democratic as well as enlightening aspirations.

References

Adams, R. 2008. *The New West: landscapes along the Colorado Front Range,* New York, Aperture.

Alpers, P. 1996. *What is pastoral?* Chicago, University of Chicago Press.

Arendt, H. 1998. *The human condition,* Chicago, University of Chicago Press.

Baudrillard, J. 2007. *Amerika,* Oslo, Abstrakt.

Baum, G. 2015. Auf dem Weg zum Weltüberwachungsmarkt. *In:* Schirrmacher, F. (ed.) *Technologischer Totalitarismus,* Berlin, Suhrkamp.

Benjamin, W. 1991. *Gesammelte Schriften,* Frankfurt am Main, Suhrkamp.

Erikstad, L. R. H., Uttakleiv, L. A., Melby, M., Lindblom, I. & Simensen, T. 2013. *Landskapstyper: metodikk for kartlegging av landskap,* Trondheim, Miljødirektoratet, Artsdatabanken, Nordland fylkeskommune, Miljøverndepartementet.

Fiskevold, M. 2016. Analysing the landscape potential in everyday areas. *In:* Jørgensen, K., Clemetsen, M., Thorén, K. H. & Richardson, T. (eds) *Mainstreaming landscape through the European Landscape Convention,* Oxford, Routledge.

Heidegger, M. 1996. *Oikos og techne: spørsmålet om teknikken og andre essays,* Oslo, Aschehoug.

Hiltner, K. 2011. *What else is pastoral? Renaissance literature and the environment,* Ithaca, Cornell University Press.

Leach, E. W. 1974. *Vergil's Eclogues: landscapes of experience,* Ithaca, Cornell University Press.

Lyotard, J.-F. 1984. *The postmodern condition: a report on knowledge,* Manchester, Manchester University Press.

Marx, L. 2000. *The machine in the garden: technology and the pastoral ideal in America,* Oxford, Oxford University Press.

Ritter, J. 1974. *Subjektivität: sechs Aufsätze,* Frankfurt, Suhrkamp.

Schirrmacher, F. 2015a. Das Armband der Neelie Kroes. *In:* Schirrmacher, F. (ed.) *Technologischer Totalitarismus,* Berlin, Suhrkamp.

Schirrmacher, F. 2015b. *Technologischer Totalitarismus: Eine Debatte,* Berlin, Suhrkamp.

Sieverts, T. 2003. *Cities without cities: an interpretation of the Zwischenstadt,* London, Spon Press.

Stahlschmidt, P., Swaffield, S., Primdahl, J. & Nellemann, V. 2017. *Landscape analysis: investigating the potentials of space and place*, Abingdon, Routledge.
Yogeshwar, R. 2015. Ein gefährlicher Pakt. *In:* Schirrmacher, F. (ed.) *Technologischer Totalitarismus*, Berlin, Suhrkamp.
Zuboff, S. 2015. Schürfrechte am Leben. *In:* Schirrmacher, F. (ed.) *Technologischer Totalitarismus*, Berlin, Suhrkamp.

Glossary

Concept A linguistically conceived object.

Idea An imaginatively conceived object. Prototypical image "and idea or eidos is the shape or blueprint the craftsman must have in front of his mind's eye before he begins his work" (Arendt, 1978:104).

Image A de-sensed, synthetic object of thought. The subjective fusion of the seen and comprehended.

Landscape Human perception of land, implying a humanity-nature relationship. The concrete result of that perception, such as a subjective image uttered in a narrative, a landscape in a painting, an area category on a map, a land description in analytical planning documents, etc.

Landscape concept A specific, linguistically conceived humanity-nature relationship.

Landscape idea Prototypical image of land symbolising a humanity-nature relationship.

Landscape ideal Prototypical image of land symbolising a desired or undesired humanity-nature relationship.

Motif The visible part of a landscape image. A motif's present visibility is an instance of confirmation. The sight of the land materialises narratives and ideals.

Motive A certain identifying and evaluating force which guides the image formation. Search for identification.

Pastoral A culture for expressing human dependence on and independence from natural and societal forces, implying a liminal state. A work within the cultural pastoral tradition.

Pastoral idea Prototypical image symbolising humanity-nature liminality.

Pastoral ideal Prototypical image symbolising humanity-nature unity, as opposed to humanity-nature alienation.

Pastoral landscape Human perception of land implying humanity-nature liminality.

Pastoral landscape idea Prototypical image of land symbolising humanity-nature liminality.

Pastoral landscape ideal Prototypical image of land symbolising humanity-nature unity as opposed to humanity-nature alienation.

Pastoral motivation Search for reconciliation guided by a pastoral ideal in an existentially problematic situation.

Pastoral motives Analytical concepts for different qualifying aspects of the pastoral motivation: emergence into appearance, discrepancy of vision, potential emancipation.

Symbol A conventional, meaningful work, such as a picture, word or site.

Vision The act of perception by means of seeing and comprehending. The result of this act.

Reference

Arendt, H. 1978. *The life of the mind,* San Diego, Harcourt.

Index

Note: Page numbers in *italics* denote figures.

absent-mindedness 16–17
accessibility, of land 8, 112
action 5–6, 8, 9, 15, 16, 20, 27, 45, 46, 51, 53, 56, 61–63, 71, 76–77, 81–82, 86, 88, 127, 135; articulated landscapes 89, 90, 92, 120, 121, 123; computed landscapes 125–129; and death 24; pastoral 125–137; reflecting on human condition 8–9; sustaining poetic potential of landscape through 3–9; and visibility of contemporary landscapes 131; visual rationality of analytical narratives 129–137
activation: of landscape ideal of insider 9–11; and landscape visibility 3, 4–5
act of seeing *see* seeing
actualisation: of landscape ideal of insider 9–11; of liminality 44, 50
Adams, Ansel 6
Adams, Robert 135
Addison, Joseph 39
aesthetic engagement: with land 51, 97, 136, 137; with nature 2
aesthetic sustainability 135–137
Alpers, Paul 4, 27, 30, 54, 55
Andrews, Malcom 44
animal laborans 97
antiquity 40
appearance, of landscape 4, 16, 25, 64; Kustein 111–113, *112*, *113*, *114*; shared 16–21; Vækerø 98–101, *100*, *101*, *102*; *see also* emergence into appearance of landscape

Arcadia 37
area(s) 7, 8; building 73, 74; clearing 73, 74; features *see* features, of land; as landscapes 7, 33, 56, 57, 64, 65, 68–75, 82, 111, 131; properties 130; protected 6, 7, 9–10; wilderness 73, 74
Arendt, Hannah 5, 53, 66–67, 70, 73, 81, 95, 98–99, 102–103, 106, 108, 128, 129
argumentation, creating landscape motifs through 71–75
artefacts: cultural heritage 43; human 73, 105, 130
artialisation of nature 50
articulated landscapes 5, 88–98, 120, 133; mutual interdependency 121–123, *122*
articulation 8; of ideal 28; of motifs 4, 18–20, 26, 66, 73, 86–87; of Sarpefossen area 74
assemblage 4, 5, 15, 21, 51, 64, 68, 74, 75, 78, 93, 130, 135
attention 78, 82, 85, 96, 121, 124, 128, 132; visual 16–17, 19, 52

backdrop 28, 86, 90, 91, 132
Bakhtin, Mikhail 78, 79
Bærum 7
Baumgarten, A. G. 42
beauty, of landscape 10, 35, 36, 37, 41, 42, 43, 135–137
Benjamin, Walter 133
biography 109
biological diversity 48

Birkenes *see* Storhei
Bjørnson, Bjørnstjerne 2, 6, 10, 15, 46
Boccaccio 37
Bodø 67, 81
body 111, 121; experiences 77, 79, 121;
   labour 113–114, 117–118; movement
   78, 79, 88, 111; reactions, Kustein
   110–111
Borregård 72, 73
building area 73, 74
bureaucracy 3, 82, 120, 126–127

Cassirer, Ernst 18, 21, 25
character, of landscape 8, 50, 90, 105,
   121, 122, 128; accentuating 107;
   Dælivannet 48; maps 49; Sarpefossen
   71–72, 73, 74; Storhei 76; Vækerø
   98–101, 103, 105, 107; Vegaøyan
   64–66, 67, 82
chronotope 78, 79, 93
civilisation 87, 88, 109, 117, 120
Clark, Kenneth 36, 37, 38–39, 79
classical pastoral models 36–37
clearing area 73, 74
co-becoming 78
cognised landscape 9
collective imagination 3
common good 76, 77
communally understood pastoral
   narratives 2
communication 8, 51, 53, 85, 134;
   and action 5; human, symbol as
   constituent 18; and symbol 18
computed landscapes: desire for
   replicability and efficiency 128–129;
   elimination of analytical critique
   through digital landscaping strategies
   126–128; invisible infrastructure
   of monitoring 126; machines and
   society's software programs 125
computerised society 54, 124, 126
conceived landscape 9
concentration, Sarpefossen 74, 75
concept, conceptualisation 8, 9, 10, 20,
   29, 37, 38, 45, 46, 49, 54, 65–66,
   71–74, 77, 79, 81, 86, 89, 91, 92–98,
   123–124, 127, **139**
conformism 52
contemplation 22, 42, 46, 56, 68,
   81, 87, 97
contemporary landscape analytical
   practice: creating landscapes within

horizon of comprehension 61–63;
   Sarpefossen 68–75; Storhei 75–81;
   Vegaøyan 63–68
contemporary pastoral analytical
   narration 50–57
contemporary pastoral landscapes
   85–86; articulated landscapes 88–98;
   giving visibility to evolving world
   123–124; image formation following
   motif articulation 86–87; material
   landscapes 88–89, 98–110; organic
   landscapes 88–89, 110–120; reflection
   of land as landscape 120–124; road,
   and shared horizon/common way of
   life 87–88
continuity: in Sarpefossen 74–75; in
   Vækerø 102; in Vegaøyan 66
contrast, in Sarpefossen 74, 75
convening: imaginative, enacted
   through words 79–81; public 54
convention 50, 51–53, 64; Edelgranveien
   91, 92; everyday landscapes 75; and
   thoughtlessness 106
Corner, James 6, 46
Cosgrove, Dennis 6, 10, 47, 49
Cosmos 38
countryside 24, 39, 41, 43
creative criticism 9
creative remembrance 92–95, *93, 94*
crisis of landscape 50
critical exchange 81
critical reflection 29, 33
cultural landscapes 2, 9, 47, 63, 64
cultural turn 10, 44
culture of vision, evolving 41–43
cycles: natural *see* natural cycles; of
   organism, visualising 113–117,
   115, 116

Dælivannet 6, 7, 8, 9–10, 15, 48–49,
   97–98, 132
Daniels, Stephen 6
death 22–24, 43, 85
decision-making 10, 47–48, 75, 77,
   105, 125, 129, 131
democracy 127
design: analytical narrative 130,
   133; landscape 46, 91, 109, 136;
   research 43–44
dialectic(s) 43, 44, 130, 136; act of
   seeing 21–26; between positive and
   negative ideals 28, 130

dialogue 22, 62; inner 55; materialisation of pastoral landscape motifs through 77–79; situated 50; between Tityrus and Meliboeus 16, 17–18, 20, 27, 28, 29, 52, 81
die Ferne 78, 114
digital infrastructure 126
digital landscaping strategies 126–128
digitised mapping 49
discrepancy, of landscape 4, 16, 45, 56, 61, 62, 81, 88; Edelgranveien 92–95, *93*, *94*; horizon 21–24; materialisation of 24; realisation 25–26; Sarpefossen 68–75; Vækerø 101–105, *103*, *104*; of vision 51–52
discrepancy of vision 18, 51–52
distance, and visual perception 28–31
diversity: biological 48; of cultural landscapes 47; of motifs 21, 70; visual, of Kustein 112, *113*, *114*, 116, 117
duality: of pastoral episode 23; world as 69
Dutch landscape 40–41

Eagleton, Terry 69
Eclogues 4, 16–20, 21, 23, 24, 25, 27, 30, 36, 37, 40, 43, 52–53, 86, 87, 124, 132, 133
ecosystem services 48
Edelgranveien 89, 130, 132; articulating a response to habitual road experiences 89; discrepancy 92–95, *93*, *94*; emancipation 95–98, *96*, *97*; emergence into appearance 89–92, *90*, *91*, *92*; as material landscape 121; as organic landscape 121–122, *123*; seasonal change 91
efficiency: and computed landscapes 128–129; productive 77
ein Mit-Werden 78
Elbe Valley 65
emancipation 4, 16, 26–31, 54, 61, 62, 88; Edelgranveien 95–98, *96*, *97*; horizon 26–27; Kustein 117–120, *118*, *119*; materialisation 28; realisation 28–31; Storhei 75–81; Vækerø 105–110, *106*, *107*, *108*, *110*
emergence into appearance landscape 4, 26, 28, 44, 51, 61, 62, 82, 85, 88, 130; Edelgranveien 89–92, *90*, *91*, *92*; horizon 17–18; materialisation 18–19; realisation 20–21; Vegaøyan 63–68; visual attention 16–17; *see also* appearance, of landscape
engagement, with land 2–3, 6, 9, 11, 24–25, 26, 29, 44, 72, 86, 88, 95, 97, 111, 115, 119, 132, 137
English landscape 37, 39, 40–41
environment 41, 44; and *Eclogues* 17, 19, 22–23; everyday *see* contemporary pastoral landscapes
environmental impact assessments 63, 77
environmental management 127
environmental planning 47
E.ON 76
episodes, pastoral 21, 23, 25, 55, 87
ethics 44, 47
Et in Arcadia ego 21–24, 25, 33, 62, 109; Chatsworth version 22, 46; Louvre version 21–22, *23*, 45, 46, 85
European Landscape Convention 2, 3, 10, 49, 54, 77, 137
everyday landscapes 41, 57, 62, 75; *see also* contemporary pastoral landscapes
existential dilemma 133
existential integrity 54
existential liminality 130, 136
experience 51, 55, 68, 69–70, 79–80, 117, 118, 123; aesthetic 38; bodily 77, 79, 121; of bodily reactions 110–111; and distance 30; and *Eclogues* 27, 29, 30; human 134; and imagination 67; personal 80; Petrarch's ascent of Mont Ventoux 38; road 89; shared 18, 65, 87, 123; and subjective imagery 25; and *Tonen* 40
expert(s) 3, 44, 56, 132, 137; -driven dialogue 78; and landscape analysis commissions 77

fabrication 98–99, 103
features, of land 8, 9, 16, 17, 36, 49; Edelgranveien 92; Kustein 111; Sarpefossen 69–70, *71*, *72*, 74; Vækerø 98; Vegaøyan 62, 66
fiction 25
fish farming, in Vegaøyan 64, 65
friction 114–115, 116

Gadamer, H.- G. 68
gardens 38–39, 40–41, 48–49
Genette, Gérard 69
Georgics 36, 37
Giorgione 36
grand narratives *see* pastoral tradition
Greece, Greek 2, 25, 37, 38, 85

Hafslund 72–73, 74, 75
hardscapes 134
harmony 26, 39, 45, 46, 50
Heidegger, Martin 81, 128, 131
Herder, Gottfried 46
heritage: cultural heritage artefacts
    43; landscape 55; pastoral 11, 129;
    see also Vegaøyan
hermeneutics 3, 51–53
Hesiod 2
Hiltner, Ken 4, 16, 19, 20, 24, 27,
    45, 132
history 8, 10, 15, 26, 30, 70, 80, 82
holistic landscape 9, 38, 49
homo faber 97
horizon 30; alternate appearance and
    disappearance of 112; dialectical
    seeing 21–24; encircling by shared
    world 17–18; entering through action
    of analyst 76–77; ever-shifting 30,
    112, 118; Sarpefossen 69; shared 65,
    87–88; and vision 111–112; visual
    evaluation of motifs 26–27
horizon of comprehension 4, 7, 8, 18,
    20, 33, 43, 45, 46, 53, 55, 85, 131;
    creating landscapes within 61–63; in
    road 87; Sarpefossen 68–71; Storhei
    76; Vækerø 102; Vegaøyan 64
horizon of motion 4, 8, 53, 55, 70, 87,
    131, 132
horizon of movement *see* horizon
    of motion
human activity 50, 53, 75, 85–86;
    monitoring, invisible infrastructure
    of 126; nodes of 73; *see also* action;
    labour; work
human condition 4, 132; landscape
    analysis as action reflecting on 8–9
humanity-nature relationship 5, 9, 10,
    27, 39, 42, 46, 62, 123, 132
Hunt, John Dixon 38, 39, 40, 43, 49, 55

idea 5–6, 8, 9, 123, **139**; cultural
    36–39; emergence into appearance

85; guiding 73, 77, 86, 87, 96, 104;
    shared 8, 9
ideal *see* landscape ideal; negative
    ideals; pastoral ideals; pastoral
    landscape ideal; positive ideals
identity 52, 108; terrestrial 109;
    translating awareness into 75–81
Idylls 2, 86
image(s) 3, 4, 5, 6, 8, 18, 23, 25,
    39, 44, 48, 55, 69, 71, 90, **139**;
    formation, following articulation
    of motif 86–87; inhabitation, and
    action 81–82; as nodes exchange
    81; shared 81, 82; subjectively
    perceived 20–21, 79; symbolic 18,
    43, 121, 123
imaginary worlds 23
imagination 3–4, 5, 6, 8, 9, 10, 20, 21,
    82, 136; capability of 131; capacities
    75; collective 3; convening, enacted
    through words (Storhei) 79–81;
    and engagement 24; and revealing
    act of seeing 29; Sarpefossen 75;
    shared 123, 133; subjective imagery
    based on worldly tensions 25–26;
    Vegaøyan 67–68
immediacy of sight, and visual
    perception 28–31
indicators of pastoral landscapes
    72–73
individual 3, 4, 5, 16, 20, 24–25, 31,
    41–42, 52, 75, 78, 80–81, 95–97,
    118, 126, 127, 133–134, 136–137
Industrial Revolution 41
infrastructure: digital 126; modern
    26, 109
inheritance 109–110, 132
inherited motives 15–31, 33, 103
inner dialogue 55
innovation 8, 51–53
insiders 42, 44; landscape ideal of,
    activating and actualising 9–11; and
    outsiders, split between (Storhei) 76
insight 4, 5, 9, 27, 28, 33, 45, 51;
    and exchange 53; methodological
    liminality 45–50; objectification
    of 135; sustainable 96, 109;
    see also sight
interpretation 3, 8, 40, 42, 51, 66, 80,
    85, 126, 130
intersubjective world 4
intertextuality 55

Jackson, J.B. 82, 86
Jonson, Ben 40
judgement 27, 45, 50, 66, 118, 122

Kant, Immanuel 42
knowledge 43–44, 78, 79, 80, 119, 120;
    legitimising, approaches to 54; and
    productive efficiency 77; shared 65
Kristiania (Oslo) 109
Kustein 89, 130, 132; appearance
    111–113, *112*, *113*, *114*; as
    articulated landscape 123;
    discrepancy 113–117, *115*, *116*;
    emancipation 117–120, *118*, *119*;
    as material landscape 123; natural
    organism, experiencing bodily
    reactions as part of 110–111;
    vegetation 114

labour 5, 8, 9, 16, 45, 46, 51, 56, 86,
    87, 88, 127, 129; and death 23;
    organic landscapes 111, 113–114,
    115, 117, 118, 121, 122
land feature *see* features, of land
landform, Sarpefossen 72
landscape architecture 6, 46, 48
landscape character maps 49
landscape concepts 49–50, 77, 86, 89,
    91, 92–95, 127, **139**
landscape idea 5, 6, 8, 36, 42, 43, 44,
    46, 53, 76–77, **139**; *see also* pastoral
    idea; pastoral landscape idea
landscape ideal 36, 42, 43, 49, 53,
    139; evanescence, stabilising 47; of
    insider, activating and actualising
    9–11; *see also* pastoral
    landscape ideal
landscape(s) 10, **139**; birth, in
    modernity 37–38; as commodity
    62; concept 77, 86, 89, 92–95, 127;
    as cultural idea 36–39; image *see*
    image(s); land reflected as 120–124;
    matters, people's participation in 54;
    modes of 24; narrative *see* analytical
    narratives; new, formation of 61–63;
    as object of planning 47–48; planning
    2–3, 10, 11, 46, 47–48, 49–50,
    56–57, 107, 110, 126–127; poetic
    potential of 3–9; as symbolic ruin
    45–47, 49
language 3, 6–8, 9, 11, 29, 39, 56, 62,
    86, 92, 123, 130

Leach, Eleanor Winsor 19, 23, 24, 25,
    26, 27, 28, 30, 62, 82, 134
legacy, pastoral 10, 40, 109
legitimacy, legitimisation 46, 47, 54, 55,
    98, 106, 120, 123, 131, 134
life 4, 5, 21, 22–24, 27, 43, 79, 125;
    conditions 20, 24, 136; everyday
    see contemporary pastoral
    landscapes; and imagination 25;
    and meaning 27
liminality 4, 9, 21, 26, 42, 127;
    analytical narratives, liminal space
    of 56–57; methodological 45–50,
    130; negotiating 43–45, 130, 135;
    pastoral 136
linguistic turn 44
locus amoenus 24, 28, 30
Loire Valley 65
Lorrain, Claude 37, 39, 40, 42
Lyotard, Jean-François 2, 54, 126, 135
Lysakerelva 110

machine in the garden metaphor 48,
    49, 125
Malmö 76
maps 48, 57, 70–71, *71*, 127–128, 130
Martini, Simone 36
Marvell, Andrew 40
Marx, Leo 20, 24, 48, 125, 128
Master 5, 6, 50
materialisation 4, 15, 62; articulation
    of visible motif 18–20; and
    interdependency of positive and
    negative ideals 24; of pastoral
    landscape motifs 77–79, 120–121;
    restorative potential of motif 28
material landscapes 88–89, 98–110;
    mutual interdependency 121–123, *122*
material resistance, in pastoral
    landscape motifs 121
meaning 4, 8, 9, 10, 15, 18, 19, 21, 33,
    46, 53, 133; and human life 27; of
    Storhei landscape 79; and subjective
    imagination 26; symbolic meaning of
    motifs 21, 26
Meliboeus 16–20, 27, 28–29, 30, 43,
    52, 53, 87, 132, 133
melody 4, 5, 6, 10
memory 6–8, 25, 28, 30, 46, 68, 88
metaphor, of landscape 29, 81; machine
    in the garden metaphor 48, 125;
    Sarpefossen 68–71

methodology, landscape analysis 3, 71,
    130; efficiency 77; independence,
    gaining 50; liminality 45–50
methods, landscape analysis 10, 11, 33,
    44, 47, 50, 52, 53, 54, 56, 69, 71, 77,
    79, 128
microscope 42
Milton, John 40
modernism 10, 47
modernity 38, 42, 79, 91, 96; birth
    of landscape in 37–38; cultural 41;
    landscape liminality 44; pastoral
    attitude 75; *see also* contemporary
    pastoral landscapes
Mont Ventoux 38
motifs 2, 3, 8, 15, 16, 17, 18, 21,
    40, 43, 51, 85, 129, **139**; capacity
    to connect vision and word 75;
    coincidental appearance of 19, 20;
    Edelgranveien 89–98; endurance,
    as symbolic statement 26–27; *Et
    in Arcadia ego* 22–23; everyday
    environments as 86; image formation
    following articulation of 86–87;
    and imagination 4; Kustein 111,
    114, 116, 117, 118, 119; and
    material consequences of choice
    96; materialisation, and positive/
    negative ideals 24; materialisation
    through dialogue (Storhei) 77–79;
    permanence and temporariness of
    20; restorative potential of 28; in
    road *see* contemporary pastoral
    landscapes; Sarpefossen 69–70,
    71–75; shared 2, 3, 29, 135;
    subjective imaginary 25–26; symbolic
    meaning of 21, 26; Vækerø 98–101,
    103, 105, 107–108, 109; Vegaøyan
    62, 65–67; visible, articulation of
    18–20; *see also* pastoral motifs
motivation 3, 4, 5, 8, 20, 28, 33,
    47, 130, 135; in contemporary
    landscape analytical practice 61–82;
    contemporary pastoral landscapes 95,
    97, 98, 103, 106–107; and pastoral
    tradition 40
motives: definition of **139**; pastoral
    see pastoral motives
Motvind 76, 78, 79, 80
movement: body 78, 79, 88, 111;
    horizon of *see* horizon of motion;
    labour of 113–114, 115, 121
myth, Arcadian 2–3, 40, 136

narrative arguments 44–45
natural cycles 114; Edelgranveien 90,
    92, 93, *93*; Sarpefossen 72, 73
natural sciences 39, 47
Nature in Norway (NiN) project
    127–128
nature reserve *see* Kustein
negative ideals 21, 23–24, 26, 27, 31,
    44, 45, 127, 130, 135; and articulated
    landscapes 94; and emancipation
    28; and episodic dynamism 25;
    interdependency of 24; and material
    landscapes 103; reciprocity and
    complementary function of 132;
    Sarpefossen 68, 69; *see also* positive
    ideals
negotiation 28, 51, 55; liminality
    43–45, 130, 135; problematic
    nature 39, 40–41; problematic self
    41–43
Norwegian Road Administration
    77, 127
nostalgia 41

objectification 42, 98, 121, 133, 135
organically evolved landscape 64–65
organic landscapes 88–89, 110–120;
    mutual interdependency 121–123, *122*
organic moment 114–115
organic reactions, in pastoral landscape
    motifs 121
Oslo 6, 7, 68, 86, 89, 98, 99, 109,
    110, 122
Oslofjord 98, 99, 109, 110, 122
Other 42, 76
outsiders 10–11, 42, 44, 76
outside world, analysis' references to
    133–135
Ovid 37

paintings 36, 40; aesthetic nature in
    38–39; *Et in Arcadia ego* 21–24,
    22, *23*, 25, 33, 45–46, 62, 85, 109;
    Renaissance 37; *Seljefløiten* (*The
    Willow Flute*) 6, 7, *7*, 15, 36, 129
Panofsky, Erwin 4, 8, 21–22, 25, 45
Paradise Lost 40
parergon 24, 88
partaking 24, 38, 97, 117, 118, 120
pastoral attitude 15–16, 30, 31, 33, 96,
    105; of modernity 75; rearrangement
    of motif 19; restorative
    potential of 134

pastoral configuration of narratives 54–56
pastoral culture 27, 64, **139**
pastoral idea 39, 46, 51–52, 74, 77, 86, 127, **139**; of modernity 91, 96
pastoral ideal 28, 29, 31, 46, 54, 56, 103, 104, 132, **139**
pastoralism 2, 20, 26
pastoral landscape idea 76, 89, 92, **140**; resilience of 97
pastoral landscape ideal 89, **140**
pastoral landscapes: contemporary *see* contemporary pastoral landscapes; definition of **140**; ideal *see* pastoral landscape ideal; indicators of 72–73; motifs, materialisation of 77–79, 120–121; restorative potential of 95
pastoral literature 19, 54
pastoral motifs 3, 19, 26, 33, 88, 91, 92, 117; appearance, diversity in 21; and bodily experience 121; departing from character of terrain 98–101, *100, 101, 102*; and discrepancy 24; emancipative powers of 28; restorative potential of 28; symbolic power of 48; updated 131–133; *see also* motifs
pastoral motivation 28, 95, 97, 130, **140**; in contemporary landscape analytical practice 61–82; essence, maintaining 98
pastoral motives 4, 15–16, 33, 61, 85–86, *122*, 131, **140**; discrepancy *see* discrepancy, of landscape; emancipation *see* emancipation; emergence into appearance *see* emergence into appearance, of landscape; inherited motives 15–31; invested in modern pastoral landscapes 39–45
pastoral tradition 4, 10, 11, 42, 61, 120, 125, 135; decline of 2; and Industrial Revolution 41; as inherited motives 15–31; literary 55; and motivation 40; newer manifestations of 2–3; view of world in 69
perception, of landscape 3, 7, 8, 9, 15, 36, 41, 80, 87, 88, 90, 102, 111, 121, 130, 134; *Eclogues* 16, 17, 18, 19, 29, 30; and modern technique 131; motifs 18–19, 67, 73; and

re-collection 50–51, 69; subjectively perceived image 20–21, 79
performance: of analytical narrative 8, 9, 82; organism, visualising 117–120, *118, 119*
performativity 124, 126, 128, 135
permanence: of land surface, visualising 101–105, *103, 104*; of motifs 20
Petrarch 36, 37, 38, 40
philosophical aesthetics 42
photographs 52, 67, 71
picture 6, 7, 7, 15, 36, 47, 48, 49, 51, 129
place(s) 3, 36, 43; and narratives 51; production, landscape as tool for 49; solitary 56; Vegaøyan 66
plurality 5; of horizons 69, 75; of visions 52; of voices 54, 55
poems 1, 2, 3–9, 10, 15, 24, 40, 42, 46, 134
poetic landscapes 55, 62; Sarpefossen 68–75
poetic potential, of landscape 68, 130; sustaining through action 3–9
polis of the eye 53–56, 80, 89, 98, 134
politics 27, 40, 48, 53, 54
Pope, Alexander 39
positive ideals 22–24, 26, 27, 31, 43, 44, 45, 127, 130, 134, 135; and articulated landscapes 94; and emancipation 28; and episodic dynamism 25; interdependency of 24; and material landscapes 103, 104–105; reciprocity and complementary function of 132; Sarpefossen 68, 69; *see also* negative ideals
positivism 3, 10, 54
Potteiger, Matthew 50
Poussin, Nicolas 21–24, *22, 23*, 37, 39, 40, 45, 85
power 24, 28, 41, 48, 79, 81, 88, 95, 97–98, 106–107, 120, 125, 133
practice(s): Sarpefossen 72–73; of travel 88; Vegaøyan 66
predictability 106, 128
Prekestolen 126
problematic nature, negotiating 39, 40–41
problematic self, negotiating 41–43
protected landscape 6, 7, 9–10
public discourse, landscape analysis in 54, 62
Purington, Jamie 50

qualities, of landscape 10, 44, 48, 116

Rancière, Jacques 56
rationality *see* visual rationality
realisation 16, 45, 62, 76, 129;
    developing subjective imagery based
    on worldly tensions 25–26; revealing
    act of seeing 28–31; subjectively
    perceived image 20–21
rebirth 21, 23, 81, 108
recollection 15, 21, 50, 69, 70; creative
    92–95, *93, 94*
re-conceptualisation of land features 69
reflection 2, 4, 51, 88, 130; critical 29,
    33; in Edelgranveien 90; on human
    condition 8–9, 132, 136; of land as
    landscapes 120–124, *122*
re-localisation of land features 69
Renaissance 37, 40, 48; Italian 2, 41
replicability 128–129, 130
representation 38, 44, 45, 48, 50, 54,
    69, 94, 128, 134, 135
restorative potential: of motif 28;
    of pastoral action 133–134; of
    pastoral attitude 134; of pastoral
    landscapes 95
restorative vision, potential for 131–133
re-temporalisation of land features 69
rhetorical response, in pastoral
    landscape motifs 120
rhetorical tool, analytical narrative
    as 55, 56
Ritter, Joachim 38, 79, 86, 97, 131, 136
Roger, Alain 50
Rome, Roman 2, 18, 24, 29, 37, 40,
    41, 82, 85
Ruff, Allan R. 41, 48

sameness 52, 104, 108, 128
Sannazaro, Jacopo 37
Sarpefossen 62, 63, 68, 70, 130;
    creating landscape motifs through
    argumentation 71–75, *72;*
    imagination 75; landscape metaphor
    68–71; map of *71*
Sarpsborg 68
Sauer, Carl 47
Saunders, Timothy 24, 29, 124
seasons 112, *113,* 114
seeing: constructive act of 16–21;
    dialectic act of 21–26; displaced/dis-
    landscaped models of 50; event of

16–17, *17;* revelatory act of 26–31,
    79, 109–110; ways of 8, 18, 48, 52,
    56, 71, 79, 88, 89, 95, 96
Seel, Martin 39
self-awareness 43, 44
self-critical reflection 33
self-understanding 41, 54
Seljefløiten (The Willow Flute) 6, 7, 7,
    15, 36, 129
shared appearances *see* emergence into
    appearance landscape
shared world 17–18
Shepheardes Calender, The 40
Sieverts, Thomas 135
sight 4, 19, 27, 30, 33, 43, 74, 80–81,
    100–101; immediacy of 28–31;
    and labour 113; methodological
    liminality 45–50; *see also* insight
situated dialogue 50
Skredsvig, Christian 6, 7, 7, 9, 10, 15,
    48, 129
society 9, 127, 128, 131, 133;
    computerised 54, 124, 126, 134;
    modern 88, 94–95, 97; and nature,
    relationship between 26, 39
solitary place 56
space 108, 134; chronotope 78, 79,
    93; between horizon of motion
    and horizon of comprehension
    55; liminal, of analytical
    narratives 56–57
speech 5, 6, 16, 18, 53, 123
Spenser, Edmund 40
Storhei 62, 63, 75–76, *80,* 130; entering
    horizon through action of analyst
    76–77; imaginative convening
    enacted through words 79–81;
    materialisation of pastoral landscape
    motifs through dialogue 77–79
Straus, Erwin 49–50, 78, 111, 114
subjective emancipation
    see emancipation
subjective imagination 3–4, 5, 6,
    8, 20, 133; Edelgranveien 95;
    imagery based on worldly tensions
    25–26; Vegaøyan 67–68; *see also*
    imagination
subjectively perceived image 20–21, 79
sublime landscape 42
subversion 48, 62
surface, of land 8, 120, 121; integrity of
    105–110, *106, 107, 108, 110;* layout

of 98; permanence, visualising
  101–105, *103*, *104*
surface of earth 66, 72, 73, 74, 98–99,
  105, 109, 115, 125
sustainability 2, 48; aesthetic 135–137
Sweco 64, 76
Switzer, Stephen 39
symbol 18, **140**
symbolic memory 25
symbolic ruin, landscape as 45–47, 49

techniques, modern 128, 131
technocratic Arcadia, impossibility
  of 48–50
technology 39, 49, 50, 128
temporality: and restorative potential
  of pastoral attitude 134; subjective
  118, 119
temporariness, of motifs 20
terrestrial fragility 118, 119
terrestrial identity 109
Theocritus 2, 86
time 74–75, 108, 109, 134; chronotope
  78, 79, 93
Titian 36
Tityrus 16, 17–20, 27, 28–29, 43,
  52–53, 87, 132, 133
Tonen (The Melody) 1, 2, 3–9,
  10, 15, 42
To Penshurst 40
topos 51
tradition *see* pastoral tradition
Trepl, Ludwig 42, 46
Trolltunga 126

Unesco World Heritage Centre
  63–65, 64
unity, humanity-nature 36–39, 42, 43,
  46–47, 49, 53, 57, 71, 72, 73, 74, 75,
  86, 89, 92, 120, 121, 123, 124, 135
Upon Appleton House 40
utopian 10, 25, 28, 44, 128
utterance 3, 5, 8, 9, 15, 16, 17, 18, 20,
  21, 24, 25, 26, 29, 43, 44, 45, 46, 50,
  51, 55, 56, 62, 66, 67, 69, 75, 76, 78,
  80, 81, 82, 85, 86, 87, 88, 114, 120,
  121, 123, 124, 127, 129, 130, 131,
  133, 135, 136

Vækerø 89, 130, 132; appearance
  98–101, *100*, *101*, *102*; as articulated
  landscape 122; confronting persistent

human intentionality 98; discrepancy
  101–105, *103*, *104*; emancipation
  105–110, *106*, *107*, *108*, *110*; as
  organic landscape 122, 123
value-free landscape analysis 47, 50, 77
Vegaøyan 62, *63*, 82; imagination
  as subjective entrance 67–68;
  institutionalised interpretation of
  130; motifs 65–67; Unesco World
  Heritage Centre 63–65
Verdensarv Vegaøyan 64
Vergil 4, 16, 19, 20, 21, 24, 25, 28, 29,
  30, 36, 37, 38, 40, 43, 55, 86, 87
Virgil *see* Vergil
virtual reality 105–106, *107*, 117
visibility 15; and activation 4–5;
  articulation of visible motif 18–20,
  73; of contemporary landscapes
  through action 131; to evolving
  world, giving 123–124; and
  imagination 3–4; of motifs, and
  human practices 121; and motivation
  4; Vækerø 100; of wilderness 74
vision(s) 9, 11, 15–16, 17, 18, 19,
  40, **140**; discrepancy of 18, 51–52;
  ephemeral character of 111–112;
  evolving culture of 41–43; plurality
  of 52; restorative 131–133; shared
  11, 53–56; transformation, in
  Renaissance 37
visual attention 16–17, 19, 52
visual evaluation of motifs 26–27
visualisation 6, 17, 19, 30, 42, 43,
  44, 55, 80, 82; accidental presence
  of organism 111–113, *112*, *113*,
  114; cycles of organism 113–117,
  115, *116*; of dynamics of landscape
  concept through creative recollection
  92–95, *93*, *94*; integrity of land
  surface 105–110, *106*, *107*, *108*, *110*;
  of modern pastoral 89–92; pastoral
  motifs, departing from character of
  terrain 98–101, *100*, *101*, *102*; of
  performance of organism 117–120,
  118, *119*; of permanence of land
  surface 101–105, *103*, *104*; of
  recurrence of concept 95–98, *96*, *97*
visual perception, language of 29
visual rationality 3, 4, 8, 15–16, 129;
  analysis' references to outside world
  133–135; landscape awareness
  129–130; updated pastoral motifs

and potential for restorative vision
131–133; visibility of contemporary
landscapes 131
vita contemplativa 68
voice(s) 3, 5, 47; of analyst, exposing
and evoking awareness 129–130;
plural 54, 55

ways of seeing 8, 18, 48, 52, 56, 71, 79,
88, 89, 95, 96
welfare state 39, 96–97
Whole of Nature 38–39
wilderness landscape 73, 74

words 3–4, 8, 19, 62; choice of 19;
imaginative convening enacted
through 79–81
work 5, 8, 9, 15, 20, 45, 46, 51, 56, 71,
86, 87, 88, 127; and death 23; and
fabrication 99; material landscapes
98, 99, 102–103, 106, 107, 121, 122,
123; and permanence 102–103, 121
Works and Days 2
world heritage *see* Vegaøyan
Wylie, John 10

zero vision 127